THE
WANTED
BOOK

THE WANTED BOOK

painted and written by

JOHN NIEMAN

Gotham Books

30 N Gould St.
Ste. 20820, Sheridan, WY 82801
https://gothambooksinc.com/

Phone: 1 (307) 464-7800

© 2025 *John Nieman*. All rights reserved.

No part of this book may be reproduced, stored in a retrieval system, or transmitted by any means without the written permission of the author.

Published by Gotham Books (March 19, 2025)

ISBN: 979-8-3485-3888-0 (P)
ISBN: 979-8-3485-3890-3 (E)

Because of the dynamic nature of the Internet, any web addresses or links contained in this book may have changed since publication and may no longer be valid.

The views expressed in this work are solely those of the author and do not necessarily reflect the views of the publisher, and the publisher hereby disclaims any responsibility for them.

Table of Contents

Introduction 11

What Would Abe Say? 13

The Right Maestro and the Wrong Man 15

Airborne Amelia 17

The Girl Who Chronicled Courage 19

The Iron Orchid 21

The Motown Man 23

Chief Nerd and Philanthropist 25

The Voice (or Perhaps Voices) of a Generation 27

One World, Thanks to Bob 29

Mr. Billions and Billions 31

Captain Cool 33

Superman Grounded 35

Go Ahead, Make My Day, and Years 37

Mr. Clutch 39

La Mome Piaf 41

Eleanor, the Activist 43

The First Lady of Song 45

The Papa of Contemporary Fiction 47

Abracadabra Success 49

Ring A Ding Ding 51

S' Gershwin 53

Jane and David Greybeard and Flo and So Many Others 55

Ms. Relatable 57

Say the Secret Woid 59

Give 'Em Hell, Harry 61

King of Nonviolence 63

"The Noble Experiment" (as Dubbed by White Writers) 65

Let's Pause for Mr. Benny 67

Dear Jack, ... 69

The One Who Rocked the World 71

Here's Johnny! 73

Bonjour Cuisine	75
The Most Atypical Movie Queen	77
So Many Larry David Moments	79
Live from New York … It's a Lorne Michaels's Creation!	81
The Iron Horse	83
Why I Still Love Lucy	85
Oh My Gandhi!	87
The Enduring Steel of Young Malala	89
Multifaceted Marie	91
The Not-So-Dumb Blonde	93
The King of Wit in America	95
The People's Champion	97
His Long Walk to Freedom	99
The Queen of Empathy	101
The Pope of the Slums	103
The World's Princess	105
The Whistle-Blower	107
Deigen Me Jugar a La Pelota	109
This One's for the Gipper	111
Rosa and the Bus	113
The Triumph of One Man's Will	115
The Man Who Taught Us to Think Differently	117
Mr. Blockbuster	119
Cowboy or President? Both!	121
The Father of Mickey Mouse	123
The Man Who Would Never Surrender	125

For Charlie

Other Books by John Nieman

Novels

The Wrong Number One

Blue Morpho

Close Call

Children's Books

The Amazing Rabbitini

Kids from A-Z

Short stories

Three-Minute Shorts

Chapters of a Life

Art with a Story

Art with a Story 2

Art Books with Poetry

Art of Lists

Art of More Lists

Art of Even More Lists

Art of Lists IV

Art with Essays

What Is Missing?

Introduction

I had just finished an art installation in Miami. It was called "What Is Missing?" Like those young missing children who were chronicled on milk cartons, this exhibition twisted the concept to missing American values, e.g., trust, innocence, live talk, role models, customer service, tolerance, and so on. It became a book.

On the heels of this, I felt like doing a sequel (sort of). This time, I chose to interpret the changing culture of America and the world with a more positive spin. "Geez, I wish there were more people around like Lucille Ball, who could always make me laugh. I want more people like Martin Luther King, who could actually inspire a nation. I want more people like Malala Yousafzai, who proved that you don't have to be a grown-up to have big ideas. I want more people like Bob Marley, who exported a local sound around the entire world. And on. And on. And on.

So the gist of this approach is the Old West wanted posters. In keeping with the dusty genre, I used four primary colors for the artwork—yellow ochre, Van Dyke brown, Indian red, and raw umber (with a very occasional splash of white). Since they are posters, the style is big, broad, and posterized.

I found I had quite a few heroes. But where does one draw the line? I ended up adding five people this last week. I could add ten more next week. The more I get into this topic, the more I discover that there is a certain indefinable push that most of them have to escape their early circumstances. True, some are gifted at an early age (e.g., Gershwin, Spielberg, and Jobs), but most go through some trial and error and then exit the tunnel even stronger (e.g., Piaf, Oprah, Disney, and Rosa Parks) ... which inspires me and makes me admire them all the more.

Enjoy. We want more of these people. No, let me correct that. We need more of these people.

What Would Abe Say?

In this cynical age of political gridlock and gamesmanship, it's worth reflecting on Abraham Lincoln. In addition to presiding over our most divisive era, the man kept his cool, stood tall on principle, and accomplished the almost impossible: he helped bring together an emotionally cleaved nation that could have easily splintered into two countries.

"This nation, under God, shall have a new birth of freedom—and that government, of the people, by the people, for the people shall not perish from this earth." (Gettysburg Address, 1863)

It was a miserable time in American history. In the 1860 election, Lincoln spoke out against slavery and swept the North but lost the South. Before he was even sworn in as president, seven Southern states formed the Confederacy and disavowed any allegiance to Washington, D.C. By 1861, the South attacked Fort Sumter, and the war between American families—North and South—was on.

More than six hundred thousand young soldiers lost their lives in this conflict ... more losses than any other war until Vietnam. Worse still, they were all Americans vs. Americans, so it was difficult to claim a victory dance on any given battle. The Emancipation Proclamation issued in 1963 was a potential turning point. As the nation approached its third year of bloodshed, it helped transform the character of the war as a fight for freedom. It also resulted in two hundred thousand black men joining the Union force.

After several battles in Richmond, where Ulysses S. Grant finally prevailed, the war did wind down, and Robert E. Lee surrendered the last major Confederate army to Grant on April 9.

An astute politician, Lincoln was reluctant to punish the South. Instead, he collaborated with Democrats and Republicans to pass the Thirteenth Amendment that, once and for all, constitutionally outlawed any form of slavery in the United States of America.

Five days after the official end of the war, the newly reelected president Abraham Lincoln was fatally shot in Ford's Theatre.

It's difficult to imagine that any other leader could have done what he did. He had a vision. He had the spine to back it up. And he had the words to inspire an entire nation, even to this very day.

The Right Maestro and the Wrong Man

He was the master of a macabre mix of wit, mystery, and misdirection. In fact, no one defined the clever, psychological twists and turns better than Alfred Hitchcock.

In the span of over six decades, the man shot seventy-five films. The first twenty-two were created in the United Kingdom, where Alfred was born and where he struggled through bad luck and several failures. At the time, he learned the trade through film title apprenticeship, silent movies, and rejection. The next fifty-plus films stamped a genre which teased and thrilled moviegoers.

The *auteur* had several idiosyncratic styles and habits. Foremost among them was a concept called "The Wrong Man." This is a plot intrigue perfected by Hitchcock. Its roots are in the red herring theory of storytelling—the viewer is lured into thinking that the evil one is Mr. X, only to later discover that those premature assumptions are 100 percent wrong. Hitchcock pushed the concept even further. In his storytelling, we eventually learn that Mr. X is totally innocent … but he is now in so deep, his only salvation is to save himself. That becomes the Hitchcock plot. The police are against him. His friends reject him. Sometimes even his family suspects him. Consequently, we can only root for him … which makes his movies particularly involving.

He was master of detail and not of fan of improvisation. Thus, he would storyboard most scenes and shoot them faithfully. In his mind, the idea was king, and not to be gambled with—it should be in the hands of the director. He also performed short cameo appearances in each of his films. Weird, but wonderful.

The canon of his output is legendary in Hollywood and in the hearts and fears of American moviegoers. They include *Dial M for Murder, Rear Window, To Catch a Thief, The Man Who Knew Too Much, Vertigo, North by Northwest, The Birds, Spellbound, Rope,* and of course, *Psycho*.

He won two Golden Globes, eight Laurel Awards, five Lifetime Achievement Awards and was eventually knighted in 1980 (despite the fact that he became a U.S. citizen in 1955). However, his biggest legacy is the lasting impact of his films. Perhaps when you go online or to a video store, you might find a package of five Hitchcock films. Buy it. Watch one. You will be hooked. And you will be surprised by the next four. Hell, you may even want to watch the next several dozens of celebrated brain and heart teasers.

WANTED

MORE PEOPLE LIKE
AMELIA EARHART
WHO CHOSE TO EXPLORE,
EVEN AT GREAT RISK TO HERSELF.

REWARDS
FOR THE ADVENTUROUS

Airborne Amelia

There are a few people in the twentieth century who had more drive, independence, or sense of adventure.

Even in her early years, Amelia Earhart was attracted to daredevil activities and had an interest in gender-bending pursuits—film, law, advertising, management, and mechanical engineering. However, when she and her father visited an airfield and she experienced her first ten-minute flight, she was hooked. As she later recalled, "By the time I got two hundred to three hundred feet off the ground, I knew I had to fly."

She soon bought a bright yellow airplane, called it the *Canary*, and flew it to fourteen thousand feet, setting a world record for female pilots.

Three years after Lindberg's first flight across the Atlantic in 1928, she became a celebrity as the first woman to cross the ocean (as part of a three-person crew). Seeking her own limelight, she became the first woman to make a solo flight across the Atlantic in 1932. She was thirty-four years old at the time, and she became a bona fide national sensation. She published books, lectured, did ads for Lucky Strike, and enjoyed a range of celebrity endorsements, which helped her finance flying.

She became friends with Eleanor Roosevelt, was an early supporter of the Equal Rights Amendment, and formed the Ninety-Nines, an organization of female pilots. After six proposals from a successful chemical engineer named Samuel Chapman, they married. Perhaps ahead of her time, she kept her own name and liked to call their union a "partnership with dual controls."

She was the first woman to fly solo from Hawaii to California. The first to fly solo from Los Angeles to Mexico City. The first to fly from Mexico City to New York. The first to fly the U.S. continent coast to coast. And the first woman to attempt to fly around the planet Earth.

Two-thirds of the way through, the flight was lost, and the exact circumstance of her disappearance remains a tantalizing mystery. She made the twenty-two-thousand-mile flight from Oakland to Miami, to South America, to Africa, to the Indian subcontinent … and then with only eight thousand miles to go, her plane disappeared in the Pacific near the Howland Islands.

Despite seventy years of searching the waters (including a multiyear, privately funded search by her husband), no evidence of the crash was ever found. However, the amazing legend of Amelia Earhart lives on and has inspired millions of ambitious women (and men) ever since.

The Girl Who Chronicled Courage

Sometimes lost in the ugly statistics of six million total deaths, one million Jewish children were killed in the Holocaust of World War II. Along with her sister, Anne Frank was one of those awful casualties. However, Anne was truly one in a million, and seventy years after the war, her impact continues to inspire young readers all over the world.

Like many upper-middle-class Jewish families in Frankfurt, Mr. Otto Frank sensed the danger of Adolf Hitler when he was elected the German chancellor. Consequently, Mr. Frank fled his homeland and moved his entire family to Amsterdam in 1933. During this period, Anne evidently loved school, wrote well, and adapted to her new Holland home.

At the risk of turning this into a history lesson, Hitler marched into Poland in 1942, and the Netherlands fell shortly thereafter. Immediately, Mr. Frank created a space above his office, behind a bookcase, where his family and a few friends hid from the storm troopers who were trying to round up all the Jews and send them to work camps or the gas chambers.

It was basically an attic with few amenities—daily food accompanied with some news reports from Mr. Frank's brave and trusted business partners who would share the events of the day. Oh, and there was one other thing. Mr. Frank gave his daughter a red-and-white booklet called a diary.

Let's stop right there. Try to imagine living for two years without any day in the sun. Think of enduring imprisonment for no crime. Think of being thirteen, fourteen, fifteen … and being an adolescent in hiding.

She wrote, she wrote, she wrote every day. Yes, there are some passages that express despair, but the vast majority of her daily essays confirm blind optimism. An example: "When I write, I shake off my cares" (April 5, 1944).

Ultimately, she was betrayed by an anonymous tip. The entire family was transported to separate concentration camps. Her mother died in the gas chambers. Her sister died of typhoid. Anne died of the same condition, two weeks before the end of WWII. Somehow, and sadly, her dad survived … and published *The Diary of a Young Girl* in 1947 as her posthumous work.

It has been printed out in sixty-two languages and continues to be the most trusted chronicle of life under constant peril of Nazi death threats.

WANTED

MORE PEOPLE LIKE AUNG SAN SUU KYI
WHO ENDURED HOUSE ARREST ON BEHALF OF HER PEOPLE.

REWARDS
FOR THE VISIONARIES

The Iron Orchid

That's what her countrymen and women called Aung San Suu Kyi for her perseverance in resisting military rule in Burma.

I have tried to imagine the ordeal. As one who has never endured imprisonment or house arrest, I cannot picture more than a few hours of confinement, without the freedom to move, speak at will, or walk around in the block. In the case of Aung San Suu Kyi, it consumed a total of fifteen years in captivity.

In 1988, after years of living abroad, she returned to her country and found the widespread slaughter of protesters who were rallying against the military junta of U Ne Win. She resisted and spoke out against it. Because of this, the government imprisoned her.

This led to her becoming a moral symbol of the inch-by-inch progress of their country (which is now called Myanmar). It's a tricky country. They would relax her imprisonment for a period … and then when unrest would reappear, they would again throw her in house arrest. And again. And again. As a result, her fifteen years of captivity were served over twenty-one years, and it proved demoralizing to the country.

In 1991, while in captivity, she won the Nobel Peace Prize.

She was finally released in 2010. However, the Burmese military continually try to sideline her or discard her. However, progress is being made, albeit slowly. In 2012, she and her political party won forty-three of forty-five seats contested in the election. Weeks later, she became leader of the opposition party. She has helped secure the release of political prisoners and the reappearance of independent newspapers.

Given the fact that soldiers by law have 25 percent of the seats of parliament, it is a slow, hard climb. However, as millions of followers believe, if there is any one person who has the perseverance, the patience, and the vision to lift the country toward democracy, it is Aung San Suu Kyi.

The Motown Man

Just think of the hits. "Mr. Postman." "Reach Out, I'll Be There." "My Girl." "Stop! In the Name of Love." "Heard It Through the Grapevine." "I Hear A Symphony." "I'll Be There." And those are just a smattering. The man produced 110 chart toppers and countless top 10 records.

His name is Berry Gordy Jr., and he launched the successful and influential era in the history of pop music. It was called Motown, and it was the carefully nurtured brainchild of this one man.

Berry was a Detroit native who boxed, served in the Korean War, and worked at the Lincoln-Mercury assembly plant. However, his true love was music. After cowriting some hits, he opened Three-D Record Mart and exposed his customers to such jazz greats as Stan Kenton, Charlie Parker, and Thelonius Monk.

However, he had bigger dreams. Thanks to an eight-hundred-dollar loan from his father, he decided to open his own record company. It became known as Motown, and the man had a gift for identifying and bringing together musical talent. Examples: Smokey Robinson (who wrote and recorded the label's first million seller). The Supremes. Marvin Gaye. The Temptations. The Four Tops. Gladys Knight and the Pips. The Commodores. Martha and the Vandellas. Stevie Wonder. The Jackson Five. Lionel Richie. And on and on and on.

His vision? To combine African-American gospel with the rock-'n'-roll sound and make it palatable to Middle America. His approach: first of all, great sound. But he also believed in carefully managing his star's public image, dress, behavior, and stage movements. As a result, the sound and look of Motown was imitated on every street corner of America in the '70s and '80s.

In 1972, he moved to Hollywood and produced several movies, including *Lady Sings the Blues* with Diana Ross. Despite much wealth and success, Motown is forever a part of his DNA. It persists to this day. For instance, in 2011, Gordy developed a Broadway show about the genre. *Motown: The Musical* ran for two years to packed houses.

If you need any further convincing, turn on the TV some late night and see those five-CD offers for Motown music. Watch for five minutes. Watch the choreography. Listen to the music. You will be hooked for the next sixty minutes. Chances are you will then call the 800 number just to rehear the music. You will not regret the choice.

Chief Nerd and Philanthropist

Unless you a true computer geek, it's challenging to fully understand the technological impact Bill Gates has had on the planet. Yes, he cofounded Microsoft, the world's largest PC software, and was its chairman, CEO, and chief software architect until May of 2014.

His tech credentials began early. Even in high school, he had consulted with many computer companies. After dropping out of Harvard, he introduced BASIC in conjunction with an IBM partnership in 1980. He introduced the first retail version of Windows five years later. For Microsoft and Bill Gates, it has been a meteoric ascent ever since.

Sometimes considered a tough, verbally combative boss, he has had success blocking competition and was even accused of being monopolistic in antitrust litigation. In his defense, computer software is difficult to protect from clone companies who wish to ride the bandwagon of someone else's success. In large measure, Bill Gates has succeeded in protecting Microsoft from imitators. It has paid off handsomely for him.

Forbes dubbed him the wealthiest man of the past ten years. He is currently the richest man in the world.

It is not a selfish wealth. After his marriage to Melinda French in 1985, the two of them formed a foundation (the Bill and Melinda Gates Foundation), which is today considered the wealthiest charitable foundation in the world. It is also considered among the most transparent charities, in terms of what goes where and what high percentage is devoted to worthy causes—mostly healthcare, extreme poverty worldwide, and an increase in education opportunities to access information technologically in the United States. Currently, the foundation appears to be worth almost thirty-five billion dollars.

In a further act of generosity, Bill and Melinda have promised that eventually they will donate 95 percent of their wealth to the foundation. I imagine that if I were one of their three kids, I might question that altruistic decision. However, as a centibillionaire, I feel assured that Bill will make sure his three offspring are provided a safe and secure future … and a belief that one must make their own path achieving the "American Dream." A rather smart lesson there. But what else would we expect of an entrepreneur who rewired the way America should move forward?

WANTED

MORE PEOPLE LIKE
BOB DYLAN
WHO REMAINS THE ANSWER, MY FRIEND BLOWING IN THE WIND.

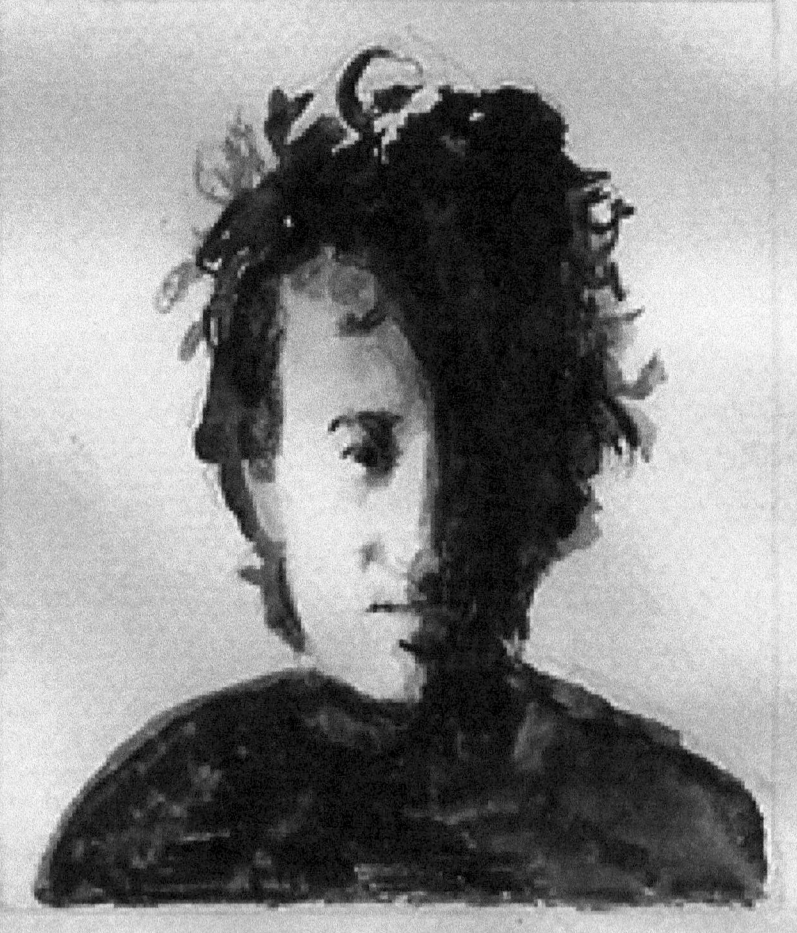

REWARDS
FOR LISTENERS

The Voice (or Perhaps Voices) of a Generation

Even as a college student at the University of Minnesota, he was attracted to folk music. Against the backdrop of rock 'n' roll, he wrote, "The songs are filled with more despair, more sadness, more faith in the supernatural. Much deeper feelings."

And so Bob tried to write both words and music that might appeal to a changing nation. Inspired by Woodie Guthrie, he moved to New York City to visit with his dying idol and try his skills in Greenwich Village. By 1963, many of his songs were labeled "protest songs," and gained wide play, including "A Hard Rain's a Gonna Fall," and "Blowin' in the Wind," which was popularized by Peter, Paul, and Mary.

Around that time, Joan Baez became his advocate and lover. With her sweet voice against his scratchy vocals, she popularized "The Times They Are A-changing" and "Like a Rolling Stone."

And yes, the times they were a-changing, as did Bob Dylan. In the early '60s, he mixed acoustics with electric guitar to the dismay of all his dedicated folkies. Despite the hit "Mr. Tambourine Man," he was frequently booed in folk concerts for his betrayal of his roots. After secretly marrying Sara Lowands in 1966, he crashed his motorcycle in Woodstock, New York, and used the accident as an opportunity to take a ten-year hiatus from live concerts. However, he did not totally withdraw from music. In 1967, he recorded *Nashville Skyline*, a hit album that veered toward country rock (including a duet with Johnny Cash). The big hit of the album? "Lay, Lady, Lay."

In 1972, he won an Oscar for his song "Knocking on Heaven's Door." In 1973, he returned to touring with the band. He recorded the big hit, "Forever Young," in the late '70s, agreed to a forty-concert tour in North America, and performed in seventy-eight venues around the world. In the 1980s, he toured with Tom Petty and the Heartbreakers, and the Grateful Dead.

Despite his multitalented styles (folk, blues, rock, movie scoring), Bob Dylan has remained an icon in all disciplines. In 1989, Springsteen saluted him at his induction in the Rock 'n' Roll Hall of Fame, saying that "Bob freed the mind, the way the Elvis freed the body." In 1997, Dylan was the first rock star ever to receive the Kennedy Center honors. He has won Grammys, Golden Globes, and Oscars.

Did he deserve all these accolades? Should we reconsider? In Dylan's own words, "Don't think twice. It's all right."

WANTED

MORE PEOPLE LIKE
BOB MARLEY
WHO TURNED A NATIONAL BEAT INTO A WORLDWIDE RHYTHM.

REWARDS
FOR ALL US WHO LIVE IN ONE WORLD

One World, Thanks to Bob

He only lived to age thirty-six, but he made a world of musical difference.

Jamaican-born Bob Marley made his mark early in life. By the age of seventeen, he had recorded four songs, including "Slimmer Down," which became Jamaica's no. 1 hit, and sold seventy thousand copies—a rather remarkable achievement on a small island.

By 1963, he formed a group called the Wailers, with some family members, and with different band members over the next decade. During that ten-year period, Marley married Rita Anderson, moved his band to Island Records, and created a growing musical reputation.

His first album for Island, *Catch a Fire*, gained rave reviews. One year later, in 1974, he recorded "I Shot the Sheriff," which Eric Clapton subsequently recorded and became #1 on Billboard's Top 100 in the same year. From that moment, Marley held on for a skyrocket career.

In 1976, he started a solo career and performed for the "Smile Jamaica" free concert, where he and his wife were shot for supposedly siding with the prime minister of this warring country. Within two days, an injured Marley returned to the stage with the opening quote, "If the people who are trying to make this world worse aren't taking a day off … why should I?"

1974, "No Woman, No Cry." A huge and emotional international hit.

1997–1978, relocation to England and the release of the album *Exodus* that perched at the top of the British Charts for 56 straight weeks. The Big Hit? "One Love."

1979, "Africa Unite." He performs against apartheid.

1980, worldwide fame. A hundred thousand people attend a concert in Milan. Two SRO shows at Madison Square Garden.

1980–1981, cancer. It spread to his lungs and brain. Given his Rastafarian religious beliefs, he rejected treatment. He died on his way to Jamaica, despite being treated as an emergency in a Miami hospital.

It was an awfully early exit for an honorable, ambitious man, who had an amazing impact in the global world of music.

Mr. Billions and Billions

As politicians like to say these days in Washington, D.C., "I am not a scientist." Their current phrase echoed my feeling as a liberal arts kid in the Midwest. However, I was scientifically riveted by a man in a turtleneck who made me feel closer to all the planets, solar systems, and possible extraterrestrials in outer space.

His name was Carl Sagan. In the 1980s, he narrated and cowrote a TV series called *Cosmos: A Personal Journey*. Each week, it connected with five hundred million people in sixty countries and is to this day the most widely watched series in PBS history.

The man had a knack for wonder and the thrill of exploration. Bear in mind, this was the era of space races, moon launches, ET, and Roswell. The idea of something beyond Earth was in the ether.

I always thought he was just an amazing entertainer. I've now learned that he was quite a respected scholar who simply had a talent for communicating his honest enthusiasm for outer space. He was a full professor at Cornell. He scientifically projected high surface temperatures on Venus. He briefed the Apollo 13 astronauts before their flight to the moon. He was awarded the NASA Distinguished Public Service Award, the Pulitzer Prize for general nonfiction, and two Emmy's.

Without a doubt, his biggest preoccupation was the possibility (he would say the probability) of extraterrestrials. And yet his enthusiasm for this position was never loony. As he once said, "The total number of stars in the universe is larger than all the grains of sand in all the beaches of the planet earth." It just made sense to him that there must be other civilizations far older and more advanced than ours. Consequently, he often experimented with ways to communicate and receive messages from those outside our own solar system.

Unlike others, he did not make us afraid of the unknown. He simply made us look at the stars and wonder. Like five hundred million other followers, I came to believe we are not alone. If I someday discover this to be true, I will have Mr. Carl Sagan to thank for the view.

WANTED

MORE PEOPLE LIKE
CHESLEY SULLENBERGER
WHO COULD KEEP PEOPLE CALM
IN THE FACE OF A CRISIS

A.K.A. SULLY
REWARDS
FOR ALL FLIERS

Captain Cool

Sometimes there is just the right person with the right skills at the right time. That was the case of Chesley Sullenberger who piloted US Airways #1549 into a miraculous, safe landing on the Hudson River on January 15, 2009.

The man was well equipped to handle a crisis, with forty years of flight experience and over twenty thousand hours in the air. Even in high school, he was identified as a member of Mensa International and then awarded a spot at the Air Force Academy. In addition, he had tons of crisis training and was actually an instructor for the airline on such things for decades.

In this particular case, striking a flock of Canadian geese during its initial climb out of LaGuardia airport disabled his aircraft. It killed both engines and resulted in one fiery blaze on his left wing. "LGA or Teterboro?" the air traffic controller asked. Instantly, Sully decided that neither one was feasible.

Instead, he got on the PA in a calm voice and told his passengers to "brace for impact." At 3:31 p.m., the plane eased down for a smooth landing on the West Side of New York City in the middle of the Hudson River. Within minutes, all the escape chutes were activated, and rescue boats were in the proximity. At the time, Mayor Bloomberg dubbed him "Captain Cool."

According to his friends and family, Chesley is shy and reticent. Consequently, he never "merchandised" the event for his own fame or fortune. As a matter of fact, he resigned from the airline within a year and simply became an occasional commentator on airline safety for CBS.

As further evidence of his humility, Sully explains the phenomenon this way: "I guess it paid off. I have been making small regular deposits in this bank of experience, education, and training."

Sully, the next time I climb out of LGA, I sincerely wish I have you at the controls, or at least someone you trained.

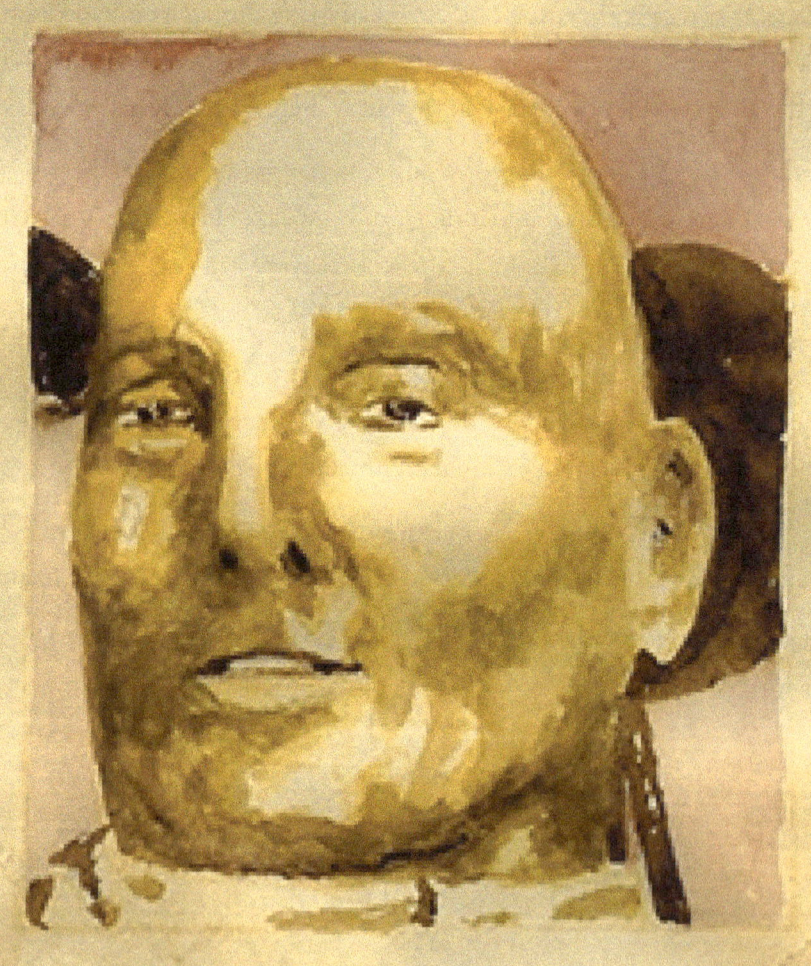

WANTED

MORE PEOPLE LIKE CHRISTOPHER REEVE
WHO PROVED THERE CAN BE GRACE IN DEATH

REWARDS
FOR THOSE WHO MOVE PAST PAIN

Superman Grounded

It's so tempting to typecast Christopher Reeve as the Hollywood Hunk who "was faster than a speeding bullet, more powerful than a locomotive, and able to leap tall buildings in a single bound." However, his impact extended beyond his *Superman* roles.

Raised in an intellectual family of some privilege, he attended Princeton Day School and excelled at sports, academics, and theater. Even in his high school, he was hired as an apprentice at the Williamstown Theatre Festival and cast in the Harvard Repertory Theatre at age sixteen. Based on his academics, he was accepted into six Ivy League colleges and decided to attend Cornell. He did well there and, in his junior year, received a full-season contract at the San Diego Shakespeare Festival. In 1973, he and two thousand students applied to Julliard. Only he and Robin Williams were selected as Julliard's Advanced Program.

Consistent with his younger successes, his professional life continued to move forward at warp speed. He starred in a Broadway play *A Matter of Gravity* with Katherine Hepburn. He auditioned for *Superman* and added thirty pounds of muscle for the role. The movie grossed three hundred million dollars in ticket sales and earned Reeve rave reviews. This was followed by *Superman II* (his favorite of the series), *Superman III*, and *Superman IV*. These were followed by *Somewhere in Time*, a romance film that costarred Jane Seymour. Then came *The Fifth of July* on Broadway and *Deathtrap* opposite Michael Caine.

In 1995, the charmed life came to a crashing halt. Chris had discovered the thrill of horse riding and trained five to six days a week. But on the third gate of a Steeplechase, his horse refused to jump, and the celebrated actor landed headfirst and shattered his first and second vertebrae. He was destined to forever be a quadriplegic, and only with extensive surgery was he able to keep his neck erect, and only by breathing through a guiding tube was he able to move his wheelchair.

After briefly considering suicide, his wife Dana encouraged him to find a new path, and did he ever! He campaigned for stem cell research and Special Olympics. He published a best seller titled *Still Me*. He won a Grammy for the best-spoken word for that book. He starred in a remake of *Rear Window* and won the SAG award for the best actor of the year. In the swell of this, he received a two-minute standing ovation at the Oscars.

Shortly thereafter, he died of cardiac arrest at age fifty-two. Many considered it an adverse reaction to antibiotics. Even more considered it a sad loss of an intelligent actor and inspirational advocate for those are who are disadvantaged through injury.

Go Ahead, Make My Day, and Years

There are few Hollywood stars that are so stereotyped in their early years and prove to be so multifaceted in later years.

Let's face it, when the guy broke onto the scene, he did look like the quintessential cowboy. Consequently, that's the image that stuck in his early years. Clint was cast as Rowdy Yates in the TV series *Rawhide* in 1961, and in the later '60s, he became "the man with no name" in a new genre of movies called "Spaghetti westerns." They were sparse, dangerous, and mysterious. They were also amazingly macho. For a reference, look at *A Fistful of Dollars*, or *The Good, the Bad, and the Ugly*.

From that launching pad, the man took a seventy-degree turn into the *Dirty Harry* series. He lost his cowboy hat and serape, but still was one man against the system. "Do you feel lucky today?"

From there, he diverted. He played opposite an orangutan in *Every Which Way but Loose*. He convincingly portrayed a tortured secret service agent in *In the Line of Fire*. He sang (badly) in *Paint Your Wagon*. He played a romantic nomad opposite Meryl Streep in *The Bridges of Madison County*. He was an aging astronaut in *Space Cowboys*.

However, his biggest later-day wallop was as a director. Who knew? *Unforgiven* was his first coup—a story that avenges rape in the Old West. *Mystic River* was a critical and popular success—an amazingly riveting story of betrayal and crime. *Million Dollar Baby* captivated millions of viewers with its painful ending (and it won four Oscars). *Gran Torino* hit us in the solar plexus. And *American Sniper* turned out to be one of the most watched films of all times.

In total, he has directed over thirty films and at seventy-four, Clint is the oldest person to win two Best Director awards. He is now over eighty years old. However, his energy seems indefatigable. Perhaps he will direct thirty more movies, or run again for mayor of Carmel. After all, he is a man of many talents.

Mr. Clutch

For twenty seasons in a New York Yankee uniform, he wore the #2. But for New York fans (and many other baseball fans throughout the nations), Derek Jeter was #1.

The guy had an infectious smile and great deal of determination in every game. Similar to Ernie Banks, he just seemed to be supremely happy on the baseball diamond. A gifted athlete since his high school days in Kalamazoo, Michigan, where he batted over .500 in his last three seasons, he was highly coveted by colleges wishing to offer athletic scholarships and by major league teams, who wanted him to play. Ultimately, he decided to pass on a scholarship at the University of Michigan and sign with the Yankees, the team he most admired.

Surprisingly, he had a rather mediocre minor league career for three years. However, by 1995, he was listed as the fourth best prospect for success in the majors. They underestimated his impact once he hit the bigs. In his first season, he hit .314 and was a postseason success when he hit that controversial home run that young Jeffrey Maier snagged in the bleachers.

The next twenty years are for the record books. He is the all-time Yankee leader in hits, doubles, games played, stolen bases, and times at bat. He was selected to the All-Star team fourteen times. He won five Golden Glove awards. When he hit the milestone of three thousand hits, it came with a home run, along with five hits at five at bats, including the game winning hit.

Not surprisingly, he was named by George Steinbrenner to be the captain of the Yankees in 2003, a title and an honor he would retain with pride until his retirement in 2014. Speaking of honor, he was the idol of many young baseball fans—at least partly because he had gone decades without any addiction other than the daily love of baseball. No steroids. No sex scandals. No gambling. No snarky rumors. No games (other than the one played between the lines).

In an era of scant role models, he remains one of very few heroes—on and off the field.

WANTED

MORE PEOPLE LIKE
EDITH PIAF
WHO MADE US ALL FEEL FRENCH WITHOUT REGRET

A.K.A. THE LITTLE SPARROW
REWARDS
FOR THE PASSIONATE

La Mome Piaf

I was in Paris a few weeks ago. Two blocks from the Louvre, I heard a street singer who was warbling "Non, Je ne Regrette Rien," It seemed to garner quite a few contributions from the appreciative pedestrians and lighten their step. Two days later, I was climbing the stairs of Sacre Coeur in Montmartre and heard another character that instinctively knew the enduring sound of Paris and played "La Vie En Rose," while coins were tossed into his hat lying on the street.

The originator of this sound was one of the most endearing, iconoclastic, and emotional performers to ever grace the streets of Paris or the concert halls of Europe, USA, or Latin America.

Her name was Edith Piaf. Despite her diminutive size (4'8"), she packed a wallop of a voice and a ton of French passion.

However, her rise to fame was not a pretty story. Her mother abandoned her at birth, and she was raised by prostitutes in Normandy, France. At the age of fourteen, she reconnected with her father, and together, they created an acrobatic street act. Soon she learned that she had the magical ability to charm the people in the streets who enjoyed her vocal range and emotional connection.

By seventeen, she was performing in the Pigalle area of Paris. Within the next ten years, she became an international sensation, performing for Ed Sullivan eight times and twice at Carnegie Hall. Of course, she had concerts in the major halls of Paris and throughout the rest of the world.

At the age of forty-seven, she died prematurely of liver cancer. However, her sound endures. Just walk the streets of Paris some afternoon, and you will hear accordionists, guitarists, and singers try their best to capture that magic.

If you have an extra euro, throw it in the hat—partly for the interpretation and partly for the inspiration.

WANTED

MORE PEOPLE LIKE
ELEANOR ROOSEVELT
WHO FAVORED HUMAN RIGHTS OVER HER OWN PERSONAL WEALTH.

REWARDS
FOR THE HUMANISTS

Eleanor, the Activist

She started her life with many advantages. She was the young daughter of wealthy, connected family. She was the niece of Theodore Roosevelt, and she was schooled well, speaking French fluently in her early teens. On the other hand, she had a very unhappy childhood. Both of her parents died before she was nine. Her young brother died in the same year. Worse yet, she always considered herself an "ugly duckling"—a taunting, whispered criticism that can be especially hurtful to a young teen. Perhaps that's why she worked so hard at an early age to become a zealous, lifelong advocate for the downtrodden.

Evidently, that's one reason Franklin Roosevelt was attracted to her. Despite his mother's stringent advice to immediately jettison the relationship, FDR persisted, and President Teddy Roosevelt walked her down the aisle to a grand wedding. Despite having six children together, their early years could best be describes as "comfortable," at best. Eleanor knew of some of FDR's dalliances with Lucy Mercer. It evidently convinced her to find fulfillment in a public life of her own. You could see some of this in FDR's term as New York governor. Eleanor's independence and activist voice became even more pronounced when Franklin was elected president in 1932.

Part of it was the president's carefully concealed polio. Eleanor became a stand-in for him on many issues. In fact, she was the first First Lady to hold a press conference (348 of them over FDR's twelve years). She was the first wife to speak at a national convention. She also was the first to have a daily newspaper column. In the process, she became the president's link to the African-American population during segregation and helped turn the New Deal into a social contract between classes.

In WWII, she visited the troops and lobbied for refugee status for displaced Jews. She also supported the all-black Tuskegee airmen and wartime women in factory jobs. Upon her husband's death (supposedly in the company of Lucy Mercer), Eleanor found a new wind. In 1945, Harry Truman appointed her a delegate to the United Nations General Assembly and succeeded in passing the Universal Declaration of Human Rights, which vehemently outlawed the WWII atrocities from occurring again (despite some significant resistance from member nations). The woman averaged 150 lectures a year. She gained thirty-five honorary degrees. Most of all, she created a different model for women in America. Through her actions, she helped American couples come to grips with the fact that women will not be silenced and may in fact have smarter ideas than their husband, even if he has the POTUS title.

The First Lady of Song

A rather shy, gawky teenager, she became the most amazing, smooth jazz voice throughout the twentieth century. Her first breakthrough? An amateur audition at Showtime at the Apollo Theatre. She was scheduled to go on as a dancer, but after seeing a breathtaking tap dancing duo before her, she decided to change her routine from dancing shoes to singing. Guess what? She improvisationally won!

Shortly thereafter, she became the lead singer of Chick Webb's orchestra and had a huge national hit, which she interpreted from a nursery rhyme, "A Tisket, A Tasket." After the bandleader died, she took over the band, which was renamed Ella and Her Famous Orchestra. Many, many hits ... but the best is yet to come.

In 1942, she recognized the changing mood of American music and moved from swing to bebop. Beyond her marvelous voice, she contributed a thing called *scat* to the sounds of the times. As she later explained, "I just tried to do with my voice what I heard the horns doing in the band." Want evidence of this innovation? Go to iTunes or YouTube and hear her original rendition of "Lady Be Good."

But wait, there's more! Perhaps her biggest contribution to American music was a series that started with Cole Porter songs, as interpreted by Lady Ella. This led to another and other, which eventually became called "The American Songbook." Album by album, it celebrated the American composer according to Ella. The subsequent albums included the amazing composition of Irving Berlin, Rogers & Hart, Harold Arlen, Jerome Kern, Johnny Mercer, and Duke Ellington ... along with other collaborative albums with Louis Armstrong, Count Basie, and Antonio Carlos Jobim.

Consider those last three or four sentences. Obviously, this woman could sing anything and create a signature style with any melody.

Until a few years before her death at age seventy-nine, she toured forty-five to fifty weeks a year and brought the joy of sound to millions of people. Mother of two, husband of three, she was troubadour of a nation for six decades.

WANTED

MORE PEOPLE LIKE
ERNEST HEMINGWAY
WHO PROVED THAT REAL MEN WRITE.

A.K.A. PAPA
REWARDS
FOR THOSE WHO LOVE STORIES

The Papa of Contemporary Fiction

For millions of literati, this one person changed our conception of what it is to love writing. Before him, there was F. Scott Fitzgerald, who dressed well and could undoubtedly mix well in the Hamptons. There was Sarah Teasdale, who was a complete recluse during her writing years. There was William Faulkner, who never liked to use periods or commas (or paragraph indentations for that matter). There was e.e. cummings, who was America's answer to haiku.

And then there was Ernest Hemingway, who was our closest thing to Teddy Roosevelt with a typewriter. The guy liked to hunt. He knew how to drink. He enjoyed travel and the adventure that came with it. He could catch big fish in Bimini. And he had a great smile that matched a great beard.

Also, the guy knew how to write and get to the point. As a young English major, I fell in love with those short sentences. They were pithy. Powerful. Punchy. Perhaps he was the first writer ever to recognize that we really do have a short attention span. We do not have the tolerance to know the exact texture of the sofa that was placed next to burl-wood desk of an insignificant character in a novel.

And yet it is a complete misread to judge him a simple writer or even a surface human being. His books, particularly *The Sun Also Rises*, *To Have and Have Not*, *The Old Man and the Sea*, *For Whom the Bell Tolls*, and *A Farewell to Arms*, are often considered by critics as some of the deepest exploration of the "Lost Generation's" angst about love, war, wilderness, and loss. (By the way, could any novelist ever write a better title?)

In the 1960s, he was sometimes criticized for his male-centric views, partially because his portrayal of women in the '40s. However, in recent years, more and more critics have begun to appreciate the strength, depth, complexity of his female characters ... or at least excuse them as symptomatic of the times.

In many ways, the man was a living contradiction. He could hobnob in cafes for months and then lose himself in writing for years. "Writing is at best a lonely life," he once wrote to his Nobel Prize ceremony (which he did not attend). He could face wild game in the plains of Africa, but often liked to surround himself with six-toed kitty cats in Key West. He could often extol the virtues of bravery in the face of fear, but ended up killing himself in Ketchum Idaho in 1961.

Perhaps because of these contradictions, we continue to be fascinated by the man, his journey, and his works.

Abracadabra Success

I refuse to attribute it all to that magical smile of his, although it is always amazingly spontaneous, infectious, and ultimately optimistic. However, Earvin Johnson has had his share of challenges along that fortunate Yellow Brick Road.

He was first dubbed "Magic" as a fifteen-year-old high school sophomore in Lansing, Michigan, where in one game he scored thirty-six points, had eighteen rebounds, and sixteen assists. At Michigan State University, he helped lead his team to the NCAA championship against Larry Bird and Indiana State, which was the most watched college game ever. In the process, Magic was named the most outstanding player of the Final Four.

The next year, he was drafted no. 1 by the Lakers and was the only rookie to win the MVP in the NBA finals. He would again win two more MVP awards, be named to 12 All-Star games, and become the all-time leader in assists per game—11.2.

That charmed life would come to screeching halt in 1991, when Johnson took his physical before the season and was diagnosed with HIV. At the time, the disease was considered a "death sentence," and it was widely assumed that you could only contact HIV it from gay sex. Johnson did a few things to change attitudes about the disease. He confessed that it came from multiple sexual partners while on the road. He reassured people that his wife and daughter were not infected. And he immediately resigned from the NBA. Over the next few years, he would toy with the idea of coming back. In fact, he did perform in the 1992 All-Star game despite the objection of several players and was awarded the MVP. He also participated in the 1992 Olympic "Dream Team. However, his career as a full-time player was effectively over at age thirty-six.

So what does one do? Fade off in the sunset? Become a recluse? Reminisce about past glories? Not Magic Johnson!

In the next several years, he became a media figure, motivational speaker, and NBA commentator, while promoting research and campaigning to lessen the stigma of HIV/AIDS. For twelve years, he spearheaded a nationwide chain of movie theaters in underserved areas, which became a significant business success. On the heels of this, he became a minority owner of the LA Lakers, investing $10 million dollars. In 2012, Magic lead a group of investors and paid two billion dollars for the Dodgers, the largest sum ever paid for a pro sports team. From that, he and his investors bought the LA Sparks, and then the LA football club.

So if you ever wonder why is this man smiling, the answer is simple. He sees the sunrise, not the sunset.

Ring A Ding Ding

He had style, sass, swing, and swagger. But most of all, the guy had song … and a very special way of delivering it.

Even in his very early days when bobby-soxers would scream for him at the Paramount Theatre in New York, he used the melodies to tell stories. Somehow, you actually felt, in your solar plexus, what the man was singing. Moreover, you couldn't help but believe that Sinatra, even at a young age, had experienced every word.

Beyond the woman vote, men identified with him and were attracted to his macho appeal. It was part-tough guy, part-carouser, and part-saloon singer. Ironically, it was also an admiration that the guy seemed to know how to walk that eternal tightrope between romantic and rascal.

After an atypical dip in popularity in the late 1950s, the icon came back with a vengeance. He signed with Capitol Records and had a string of amazing hits, despite the advance of rock and roll. He collaborated with Antonio Carlos Jobim, Count Basie, and Nelson Riddle. He made a string of interesting movie (including *From Here to Eternity*, which earned him an Oscar). He created the Rat Pack. He was a JFK buddy. He wore his hat cocked, a raincoat over his shoulder, and invited people in auditoriums to "Come Fly with Me."

I wanted to be just like him, and I remember the first time I ever saw him perform. It was in St. Louis at Kiel Auditorium. I think it was 1978. I was in my late twenties, and probably one of the youngest audience members. I remember when the man walked onstage in the tuxedo with an orange pocket square. The crowd went nuts. I wondered how he would silence them. He did it in three or four seconds. He took the mike and sang, "I've got you … under my skin." From wild applause, it went to total silence as every audience member wanted to hear every phrase.

The guy always had a knack for stopping you in his track and making you reconsider whether your solitary life really is the answer. Every once in a while, I need it. Every once in a while, you do too.

S' Gershwin

Just listen to "Rhapsody in Blue."

Earlier today, I wrote a full glowing profile of this prolific talent. Tin Pan Alley. "American in Paris," "Porgy and Bess." Someone to Watch Over Me." "Embraceable You." Amazing songs for movies. Early death at age thirty-eight.

And then I listened for the umpteenth time to "Rhapsody in Blue." It sums up everything! Pathos. Passion. Mood changes. Sadness. Soaring love. The rush of traffic. Loneliness. Conflict. Heroism.

Just listen to "Rhapsody in Blue." Maybe every morning.

WANTED

MORE PEOPLE LIKE
JANE GOODALL
WHO DISCOVERED THAT CHIMPS ARE NOT SUCH DISTANT COUSINS.

REWARDS
FOR THE WILD ONES AMONG US

Jane and David Greybeard and Flo and So Many Others

For fifty-five years, the woman interacted with chimpanzees in the Gombe Stream National Park in Tanzania ... and forever changed the knowledge of how humans might relate to their primate relatives.

Born in London, young Jane was given a lifelike chimpanzee doll, which she adored, and still has on her dresser to this day. That, and a keen interest in anthropology seemed to propel her in her life. In her early twenties, she went to Africa and studied primate behavior with her mother. With the help of her sponsor, Louis Lehey, she was accepted at Cambridge and gained her PhD, detailing her first five years in the Gombe Reserve of Tanzania.

Her approach was drastically different from academics that had preceded her. For one thing, she lived in the jungle with the chimps. Secondly, instead of numbering them like science test tubes, she named them according to their individual personalities—a unique idea at the time. They were known as David Greybeard, Goliath, Mike, Humphrey, Gigi, Mr. McGregor, Flor, Fredo and many others.

In the process, she observed joy and sorrow, hugs, kisses, pats on the back, and tickling. Her discoveries changed scientific perceptions in two ways. Until her life with chimps, we thought only humans could use tools and that chimps were vegetarians. She learned that they could strip off the leaves of branches and use them as weapons. She also discovered that, like humans they were capable of aggressive behavior. For example, they were quite capable of killing smaller primates like colobus monkeys and imbibing them.

To this day, Jane Goodall is the only human ever accepted in chimpanzee society. In 1977, she formed the Jane Goodall Institute, which supports Gombe research and has nineteen offices around the world. She has also created a global youth program called Youths and Shoots that has ten thousand groups in more than one hundred countries and studies conservation and development programs in Africa.

Twice married, Ms. Jane Goodall to this day travels three hundred days a year on behalf of her beloved chimpanzees and the environment.

Ms. Relatable

I think it was an afternoon in 1990. At the time, I was not quite sure why I went to her lecture in Manhattan.

I was not in a personal crisis with some girlfriend who "wanted her own space." I was not a mindless liberal who wanted to join the let-us-all-have-an-abortion brigade. If there is any possible explanation in retrospect, it was probably because I was a mad man/advertising guy who just wanted to eavesdrop and try to better understand how to sell sanitary napkins and Campbell's Soup and Crest Toothpaste to the womenfolk who went to the grocery stores with a checkbook every week.

Ms. Gloria Steinem gave me an earful. In the process, I was impressed, and what she had to say forever changed my view of women in the workplace, marriage, and the prospects for my daughter (and sons) I would someday have.

A Phi Beta Kappa graduate of Smith College, Gloria had previously exposed the Playboy myth with an article called "A Bunny's Tale," which revealed (in full costume) the working conditions and sexual demands of Hugh Hefner's Clubs. In recent days, with the help of *New York* Magazine, she had founded *Ms. Magazine* with a wondrous, modernized *Wonder Woman* on the cover. The test run of three hundred thousand copies sold out in eight days.

I listened to her.

"Yes, this is good for women."

"But I also submit to you that it is good for the men in this audience *(somehow, I thought she may have been looking at me)*. At some point, your wife will have a baby. And *unlike today*, you will be able to witness that birth … and maybe gain a few weeks off to care for her and learn to love your baby. You might actually be able to attend a school conference. Attend a soccer game, or a girl scout meeting."

To all the men who may read this, you may think, so what? Of course, we all do this! Well, guess what … we never did this until Gloria Steinem challenged us to give women equality in the workplace, and men equality on the home front.

Thanks, Gloria. Over the last few days, I have thought about your influence on me.

Today, I no longer wonder why I attended your lecture as a curious twenty-something guy. Through the journey of this essay, I hope you know you made me a better man.

WANTED

MORE PEOPLE LIKE
GROUCHO MARX
WHO DEFINED QUICK WIT
WITH A LOVABLE, LEERING LOPE.

REWARDS
FOR THE FUNNYBONES

Say the Secret Woid

There are a few more idiosyncratic entertainers than Groucho Marx.

For one stupid thing, he has probably inspired more Halloween costumes than any other hero or superstar. They are called "the Groucho Glasses"—composed of dark eyebrows, big nose, and thick moustache and black glasses. Add a cigar and stoop at the waist, duck walk with your right hand behind your back ... and people will mimic. "You bet your life." This remains despite the fact that the man passed from this earth thirty years ago.

Like many of the early twentieth century, Groucho and his brothers got their start in vaudeville. However, the jump start was at the Palace Theatre in New York City. Shortly thereafter, they were discovered by Hollywood and made twenty-six zany movies—including *Cocoanuts, Animal Crackers, Monkey Business, Horse Feathers, Duck Soup,* and *A Night at the Opera.*

In all of these movies, Groucho's innuendo-laden patter (mostly with Margaret Dumont) delighted audiences as much as his physical humor. Based on his wit and verbal skills, he was cast as the host of a TV game show called *You Bet Your Life.*

It was barely a game show, with such puzzling question as "Who is buried in Grant's Tomb?" and "Can you name the color of the White House?" No, it was a platform for Groucho's wit and repartee with regular people. Example with contestant Charlotte Story:

Charlotte: I have borne nineteen children.

Groucho: (after a take) Why so many kids?

Charlotte: I love my husband.

Groucho: (with a wink and a leer to camera) I love my cigar too, but I take it out of my mouth every once in a while.

The man remained one of the most revered icons in America. In 1974, Jack Lemon presented him an Oscar for Lifetime Achievement. To this day, you will see those Halloween costumes at grown-up parties. If so, ask the person to "say the secred woid."

Give 'Em Hell, Harry

Perhaps I just have a soft spot in my heart for underdogs. If ever there was one in the United States presidency, it was Harry S. Truman (incidentally the *S* stands for nothing).

In FDR's fourth term with WWII still on the battlefields and aware that he might not last the entire term, Roosevelt anointed Truman as his vice president over left-winger Henry Wallace, who had served as Veep since 1940. At the time, Truman was a relative unknown plain talker, who had been promoted by Boss Prendergast of Kansas City, but had demonstrated some independence from the Democratic machines since he had exposed waste, fraud, and corruption in wartime contracts.

Evidently, he met with Roosevelt only twice after the 1944 election. And then lo and behold, only eighty-two days after the election, FDR dies of a coronary, and Mr. Unknown, Mr. Harry Truman becomes the thirty-third president of the United States. What a time to become the beacon of the free world!

Within two weeks after assuming the presidency, the Nazis surrendered in Europe (in fairness, this was already in the works). But none of the following was in the works:

America's funding of the United Nations
The Truman Doctrine to contain communism.
The controversial atomic bomb drops in Hiroshima and Nagasaki, which saved 250,000 to 500,000 lives (according to Truman and his advocates)
The Thirteen-Billion-Dollar Marshall Plan to rebuild war-torn Europe
The Berlin Airlift
The creation of NATO.
The American support of Israel
Desegregation of all U.S. Armed Forces.

But my favorite Truman act of courage was in the 1948 election, when nobody thought he had a chance to win. In defiance, he went on a whistle-stop tour along the railways and seemed to gain steam along the way. But every research organization had already assumed he was dead meat. In fact, the night of the election, the *Chicago Tribune* prematurely flashed the headline, "Dewey Defeat Truman."

How could the media be so wrong and Truman be so persistent? (1) All the polls were conducted by telephone at the time, and most democrats (especially supporters of Truman did not have this newfangled device), (2) he just believed. When people used to scream out, "Give 'em hell, Harry." He would answer, "No, I just tell the Republicans the truth, and they think it's hell."

Add to that my favorite executive plaque of all times: The Buck Stops Here.

WANTED

MORE PEOPLE LIKE
MARTIN LUTHER KING, JR.
WHO HAD A DREAM
THAT INSPIRED A NATION

REWARDS
FOR ALL DREAMERS

King of Nonviolence

Without a doubt, he did more to advance racial justice in this country during the twentieth century than any other man. He did it without firing a single bullet. Instead, he used the power of rhetoric, marches, sit-ins, and prayer.

For Martin Luther King Jr., it ended up being a lifelong mission from his college days. Along the way, there were wiretaps, harassment jailing, and death threats. Of course, the quest ended prematurely with King's early assassination in 1968.

His first activist movement was related to Rosa Park's refusal to move to the back of the bus. With NAACP leader E.D. Nixon, King helped lead a 382-day boycott of busses. Eventually, the city of Montgomery lifted its prejudicial law. The remainder of his life was devoted to racial justice.

In order to call attention to the cause, he organized "sit-ins" in the early '60s. In twenty-seven cities, young African-Americans would refuse to move from the segregated lunch counters, and were often subjected to verbal and physical abuse. King himself was arrested in the Atlanta sit-in. (The city dropped the charges, fearing bad publicity.)

In Birmingham in 1963, MLK organized a demonstration that involved families. Police turned dogs and fire hoses on the demonstrators and jailed Martin and a large number of his supporters. However, given the awful TV images, nationwide public sympathy was beginning to turn. It took a major upward swing a few weeks later when in the shadow of the Lincoln Memorial, King gave his "I have a dream" speech. Two hundred thousand people attended and were moved. The rest of the world cheered on TV. The result: the 1964 Civil Rights Act.

In 1965, in Selma, police met protestors on the Edmund Pettis Bridge with nightsticks and teargas, hospitalizing seventeen marchers. King was not there at the time, but did attend the March 9 march with 2500 marchers who met the barricades and responded by kneeling in prayer. This aroused support for the 1965 Voting Rights Act.

The journey continued with a campaign against poverty, but was cut short when an assassin's bullet ended his life on a hotel balcony in Memphis. Immediately following this tragedy, there were riots and demonstrations in more than a hundred cities. Years later, there is the enduring difference that the man made in racial equality. As everyone in this country knows, there are still miles to go, but the country could never have come this far without the inspiration of Dr. Reverend Martin Luther King Jr.

WANTED

MORE PEOPLE LIKE
JACKIE ROBINSON
WHO BROKE THE COLOR BARRIER IN BASEBALL

REWARDS
FOR EQUALITY-ORIENTED FANS

"The Noble Experiment"
(as Dubbed by White Writers)

He was the first and arguably the most able baseball player to break through the color barrier in Major League baseball ... despite racial slurs, protests, and personal indignities.

Three facts that should be considered throughout this essay: (1) Jackie Robinson was a world-class athlete, (2) he had to suffer curses along the way, (3) there were heroes and villains on his path to success.

Let's go back. At UCLA, he earned letters in four sports—baseball, basketball, football and track & field, (the first athlete to do so). In 1942, as a WWII volunteer, he was assigned to a segregated troop, i.e., blacks only, in Fort Riley, Kansas. After service to his country, he was the first African-American drafted into the Major League Baseball since 1880.

Branch Rickey of the Brooklyn Dodgers deserves some credit at this point. The baseball executive determined that Robinson was the one guy who could prevail against the racial abuse that would be directed at him. In their negotiation, Mr. Rickey sympathetically told the star that he would have to "turn the other cheek" to inevitable abuse. Despite an immense amount of pride, Jackie did so for the cause.

After a few years in the minors, he joined the Brooklyn Dodgers in 1947, at the rather ripe age of twenty-eight. In his first season, he led the league in stolen bases and was named Rookie of the Year. The next year, he led the majors with a batting average of .347 and was named the most valuable player.

It was not all roses. Some Dodger players insinuating they would rather sit on the bench than play alongside Robinson. Leo Durocher, the Dodger manager, invited those who did not want to play to "leave the team, here and now." In St. Louis, the Cardinals threatened to strike. Often, he was not allowed to stay in the same hotels or eat in the same restaurants as his teammates.

And yet he persisted. In ten major league seasons, he starred in six World Series. He played in six all-Star games. He hit .311 in his career and scored over one hundred runs in six seasons.

Beyond the Hall of Fame and other national, presidential honors, his jersey number (42) was retired by the Brooklyn Dodgers, and has subsequently been retired by every major league baseball team. Since 2007, every player of every major league baseball team wears the number 42 on April 15 as a tribute to the man who had the guts, the talent, and the perseverance to forever change the complexion of baseball.

WANTED

MORE PEOPLE LIKE
JACK BENNY
WHO COULD APPRECIATE A PAUSE.

REWARDS
AND SMILES

Let's Pause for Mr. Benny

I'm not sure Jack Benny could fit in today's comedy scene. Wait a minute! I'm not sure he should have even fit into the comedy scene of fifty years ago.

That's what makes this impresario such a miracle! Unlike all the vaudeville guys, slapstick clowns and rat-a-tat punch lines, this proud man was distinctly different.

For starters, he always looked as if he walked out of Bloomingdale's with an unlimited American Express card … and yet, the running gag had everything to do with miserliness. He built a reputation as the cheapest man in America. Perhaps we should call that a thirty-nine-year schtick, since Jack always claimed to be only thirty-nine, despite being twice that age.

However, his biggest contribution to comedy was "the take," or "the pause." Rather than one-up his costars, Jack preferred to let it all sink in, and then come back with the perfect retort. Sometimes it would take a few seconds. Sometimes it would even take a repeated question.

Example: Burglar comes up to Mr. Benny in a TV sketch holding a gun to his chest.

Burglar: Your money or your life!

Benny: (no answer)

Burglar: (incredulous, and even more impatient this time). Your money or your life!!

Benny: (after another two-three second pause). I'm thinking about it!

Jack enjoyed decades of popularity on radio, and fifteen years at the top of his game on a weekly TV series. Unlike many segregated performance acts of the era, he broke racial barriers with his sidekick Rochester, who was not above gentle jibes at Mr. Benny, particularly about his supposed cheapness.

Another running gag: the fact that Jack liked to carry around a violin and occasionally play "Love in Bloom." I know it doesn't sound funny, just bizarre … but that's what made it so nutsy. Just watch reruns of *Johnny Carson* some night, and see the admiration that many comedians had for Jack, as they would slowly stare at the joke and then raise their hand to their cheek and finally say, "Well."

Maybe you had to be there. But I truly doubt it.

Dear Jack,

I wish I had met you. Despite that unfortunate disconnection, I feel like I know you very, very well.

Maybe that comes from being a child of the '50s and '60s, and discovering the new face of optimism, wit, and intelligence … all wrapped up in the most charismatic American president ever.

I know, I know, I know … you screwed around with bimbos, and undoubtedly had to do some "deals" to move this country forward. For the sake of this essay, let's concentrate on the less salacious stuff. As a young boy, I studied your military service. Amazing! On PT-109 in the Salomon Islands, your boat was destroyed and you ended up saving the entire crew—including one guy you swimmingly towed with a life vest strapped to your teeth, despite a chronically weak back. So you get the navy and marine corps medal for "extremely heroic conduct, etc., etc.…" And you are a bona fide war hero.

Within the next fifteen years, you became a congressman, senator, a vice presidential nominee and a presidential contender. Let's fast forward to the razor-thin election of 1960. I watched the debate. It wasn't even close. I know … people who listened on the radio thought Nixon had won. Welcome to television!

Along the way, I followed the Bay of Pigs Invasion, and watched the Cuban Missile Crisis in my Midwest living room while my mom was in tears about the possible "destruction of the United States." "I pray for the president," she told me. And then came the Peace Corps. Your speech in Berlin, "Ich Bein ein Berliner," before a million people in the Streets. The space race. Civil rights progress.

Unfortunately, a bullet in Dallas ended the promise of Camelot.

Fifty years later, I still don't think I have recovered. I think it could have been truly great. Let me correct that. I think for a few years, it truly was great.

I continue to hold out hope that it can be again.

Your friend, John

The One Who Rocked the World

"You may say that I'm a dreamer, but I'm not the only one," so said John Lennon in his song, "Imagine."

Let's face it, the world's most influential rock band would have never been created without him, or went its independent ways without his wanderlust.

From a hardscrabble youth in Liverpool, he took up the guitar and formed a band called the Quarrymen, which in 1960 transformed into the Beatles. With the help of Paul McCartney, they hired fourteen-year-old lead guitar prodigy called George Harrison, and with drummer Pete Best gained a contract in Hamburg. They renewed for two more seasons, at which time Ringo Starr became the new drummer, along with the song "Love me Do," which became #17 on the UK pop charts.

The rise from there was meteoric. Suddenly, Europe discovered them, and Ed Sullivan wanted them in prime time American TV. It was absolute mayhem. Every album they created topped the charts and endeared them to screaming fans. Make no mistake: it was not just a pop phenomenon. They were groundbreakingly good. They created twenty-five #1 singles, and sold out concerts everywhere.

Ultimately, John argued to take the group in studio, since the quality of the music was distorted by the audience enthusiasm. After only one decade of the Beatles and two years of a relationship with Yoko Ono, John Lennon expressed a desire to break away from the group. Many consider the break-up a liberating experience for John Lennon. He released "Imagine" in 1970, which became an anthem for the antiwar movement.

On December 8. 1980, a young disturbed man named Mark David Chapman shot him four times in the back, after Lennon had signed his new *Double Fantasy* album for the guy in front of the Dakota apartment building. The world mourned. Strawberry Fields in Central Park was installed in his honor. I remember being in Soho with crying people in the very morning of this tragedy.

"I hope someday, you'll join me … and the world will be as one," John Lennon prophetically sang. *"Imagine."*

WANTED

MORE PEOPLE LIKE
JOHNNY CARSON
WHO WAS INVITED INTO MILLIONS OF BEDROOMS FOR DECADES.

REWARDS
FOR THE LIGHT-HEARTED

Here's Johnny!

For thirty years, he was a nightly necessity for millions of Americans … and water cooler talk the next morning.

The guy had a knack for connecting with middle class America, as well as the people in Malibu, the Upper West Side of Manhattan, Palm Springs, and course, Hollyweird.

In an increasingly polarized world, it's almost impossible to imagine anyone uniting us in laughter as he did.

The show was called *The Tonight Show*, and Johnny was certainly the most celebrated, highly-paid and most contradictory of all the men and women who ever sat in that chair. Widely known to be extremely shy off-camera and even socially uncomfortable, he was the picture of ease behind that desk.

Trained as a young magician ("The Great Carsoni" at age fourteen), he did eventually follow the trail from Nebraska to Hollywood. From the beginning, his show was a hit. In addition to his monologues, his comic characters like Art Fern, and Carnac, the Magnificent delighted audiences.

However, by almost anyone's assessment, his biggest talent was making guests feel comfortable and welcomed in their debut. In this regard, he applauded and introduced David Letterman, Jay Leno, Jerry Seinfeld, Ellen DeGeneres, Tim Allen, Joan Rivers, Drew Carey, and countless others to showbiz fame.

In 1992, Johnny announced his retirement from the show in this way: "I am taking the applause sign home tonight, and putting it in the bedroom."

At the age of sixty-six, he retired on top, and suggested that he might someday return for a special or two, if it truly captured his imagination. Evidently, it did not. As a former magician, he basically disappeared from sight for the next thirteen years, perhaps adding to his mystique. However, he will always be revered and remembered by those who tuned in every single night.

Bonjour Cuisine

Julia Child, in my opinion, entertained, and educated American taste buds more than any other person in the twentieth century,

Let's face it. She was an atypical TV personality. In a world of contemporary social media, she was not exactly Kim Kardashian. However, the woman did know how to cook. And she did know how to communicate. She also knew how to capture the thrill of a meal, and the satisfaction of sharing it with loved ones.

She was trained as an elite brainiac. After attending Smith College, she moved to New York, and worked for four years in advertising, PR, and journalism.

After WWII, the woman attended the Cordon Bleu, and joined the Woman's Club Le Circle as kitchen staff. However, her biggest leap happened in Paris when she joined two other women culinary mavens—Simone Beck and Louisette Bertholde. Julia was the one who could make the cuisine palatable and relatable to millions of Americans. Their first output was a 726-page manuscript called *The Art of French Cooking*.

It became a best seller. And this led to a one of the first-ever TV shows on television. It was first broadcasted in Boston on WGBH, as *The French Chef* in February of 1963. She was not the first televised chef, but she was the most widely seen chef ever on TV. In the process, she earned Peabody Awards and Emmy Awards. There were twenty books based upon the TV show, and there were millions of meals created in St. Louis, Philadelphia, Newport, Charleston, Atlanta, Sarasota, Phoenix, and dozens of other American cities. So we learned beouf bourguignon, soupe a l'ognone, veal blanquette, and crème brulee. *Bon appétit*!

Julia died in 2004 at the age of ninety-two. If she could have lasted another day, I would love to know what surprise she may have presented on the plate tomorrow.

WANTED

MORE PEOPLE LIKE
KATHERINE HEPBURN
WHO ALWAYS PLAYED STRONG
WOMEN BEFORE IT WAS IN VOGUE.

REWARDS
FOR THE TRAILBLAZERS

The Most Atypical Movie Queen

I always thought she was one of the most attractive women in all of Hollywood, not because she could bat her eyes bigger than the bimbos, or sashay across a restaurant more suggestively than the constant auditioners. No, what was most striking about Kate was that she was never afraid to mix it up with men, and compete with anyone on wit, wisdom, and wiles.

In the early days, it did not always serve her well. She was often viewed as diffident and challenging. In time, those were the very characteristics that made her the most celebrated actress in the twentieth century. As a matter of fact, in 1999, she was named "the greatest female star in the Hollywood history."

But I get ahead of myself. Like many icons, she bounced back and forth between success and dry periods, often balanced by a north star of commitment. Her first Oscar came early—in 1933 opposite Cary Grant in *Bringing Up Baby*. After a drought of thirty-four years, she won her next in 1967 for *Guess Who's Coming to Dinner* (opposite a dying Spencer Tracy). Then one year later, she won again for *Lion in Winter*. In 1981, she won her fourth for *On Golden Pond*.

In the history of the Academy, no one has ever won more Oscars, and yet she never attended a single ceremony. As she once said, "As for me, prizes are nothing. My prize is my work." And did she ever work! She constantly alternated between Broadway, movies, and even TV as a way to stay energized and sharp.

She did have a very private north star—a twenty-seven-year legendary love affair with Spencer Tracy. They appeared in nine movies together, where the two of them perfected a newfangled concept called the "Battle of the Sexes." She would wear trousers and take no guff from him. He would sigh and fume, and occasionally argue back. And yet there was always obvious affection … sort of like a real marriage. Except it wasn't. Given the times, it was always hidden from the public, even when Tracy died, and Kate declined to attend the funeral out of respect for his long-separated wife and his children.

She was an amazing, talented woman. In view of her private life, I might even go so far as to call her noble … an accolade few Hollywood stars could ever earn.

So Many Larry David Moments

I absolutely defy you to get on a transatlantic flight, hit the "Curb Your Enthusiasm" button, and *not* disturb your new neighbor/stranger in seat 42 B with audible laughter. The guy is on the screen that awkward, that embarrassing, and ultimately that funny.

We all have our "Larry David Moments"—when we open our trap and just say the worst possible thing at the worst possible moment. Somehow in Larry's episodes, the situations just get worse and more absurd. That's at least part of the appeal. If he only had the humility to say that it was all one big misunderstanding … but then it wouldn't be "Curb Your Enthusiasm," would it?

Perhaps because Larry David plays the character named Larry David in the show, he named all of his cast members by their real first name. Or was it just laziness? The ensemble cast was excellent: Cheryl Hines (who plays Cheryl), Jeff Garland (who plays Jeff), Susie Essman (who plays Susie), and featured players such as Richard Lewis, Wanda Sykes, and Ted Danson (who play themselves).

Unless you live in a cave, you undoubtedly know the appeal. If not, here are a few classics to download:

"The N Word," where he is overheard retelling a story from a coworker who uses a racial slur, only to be overheard by the black family who is living with them. Yes, they assume Larry privately uses the "N" word.

"Denise Handicap," Larry in his single days gets a date with a beautiful woman and subsequently discovers that she is confined to a wheelchair. When he discovers such newfound respect for his generosity in dating "someone in that condition," he simply wants to date more paraplegics.

"The Pants Tent," where he thinks his trousers suggest an erection, and so does his wife's best friend.

"Mary, Joseph, and Larry," where he tries to dispel the stereotype of tipping people unevenly during the Christmas season, he decides to hire a live cresh with disastrous results.

"The Grand Opening," his new restaurant and new Tourette syndrome chef basically tells everyone to F off, and Larry decides to join the crowd.

Before that, he wrote seven amazing years on *Seinfeld* and many more years of comedy writing and stand-up performances. An amazingly funny guy, who finally found his voice and his audience in modern America.

Live from New York …
It's a Lorne Michaels's Creation!

He had a boyhood in Toronto, Canada, and God willing, he may have many years later in life as he looks out over the Western sunset. However, nothing defines this man's passion and output more than the forty-year miracle called *Saturday Night Live*.

For so many millions of people, it has been a "must-see" staple as we approach the witching hour on the last night of the week. Often uneven, sometimes brilliant, the show has been the irreverent poke at pop culture, politics, and off-center satire week after week after week.

It is the undeniable brainchild of Lorne Michaels with a trusting assist from Dick Ebersol, who was running NBC night programming at the time. On the strengths of Lorne's credits as a "laugh-in" writer and Lilly Tomlin as producer, Ebersol green-lighted the idea for a weekly live comedy show. Lorne spent five months casting a group of relative unknowns: Chevy Chase, Dan Akroyd, John Belushi, Jane Curtin, Larraine Newman, Gilda Radnor, and Garrett Morris. They were called the "not ready for primetime" players. The first show on October 11, 1975, was hosted by George Carlin and became an instant hit.

In the ensuing decades, hundreds of shows have had the same effect, and launched some of the greatest comedic talents in America. Want names? Eddy Murphy. Bill Murray. Christen Wiig. Adam Sandler. Mike Myers. Seth Meyers. Dana Carvey, Billy Crystal, Nora Dunn. Jimmy Fallon, Al Franken, Bill Hader, Darrell Hammond, Phil Hartman, Julia Louis Dreyfus, Jon Lovitz, Tim Meadows, Dennis Miller, Tracy Morgan, Kevin Nealon, Amy Poehler, Andy Samburg, Tina Fey … and scores of others.

The show has featured many of the best musical guests in the world, and skewered politicians on each side of the aisle, but its greatest accolade is longevity of laughter. As Lorne Michael once said in 1990, "At twenty-five, I could stop now, and be good." However, he has continued to amuse us for more and more and more years. Along the way, he has been nominated for 156 Emmy's (winning thirty-six of them), produced many movies and TV shows, but every Saturday night, he captures the attention of millions of viewers. Once we hear the refrain, "Live from New York," we know we are in for a wild, spontaneous ride.

The Iron Horse

Unlike so many arrogant sports stars of today, Lou Gehrig was a quiet hero. He performed admirably for the New York Yankees from 1923 to1939. During that era, he excelled in six World Series championships, seven all-star games. In the process, he won two American League MVPs, and had a batting average at a remarkable .340 and an on base percentage of .447. In the midst of all this, he played 2,137 uninterrupted games … a feat that was only eclipsed recently by Cal Ripken Jr.

However, despite his achievements, he is probably best known for his demise. At the age of thirty-six, he sensed a diminution of his athletic prowess, and asked his manager to "bench" him. Within the next two years, he was diagnosed with ALS (which later became commonly known as Lou Gehrig disease).

On July 4, 1939, to a sold-out stadium on an event called "Appreciation Day," what is Lou stood before a packed house at Yankee Stadium, and said:

"Fans, over the past two week, you have been reading about the bad break I got today. I consider myself the luckiest man on the face of the earth. I have been in the ballpark for seventeen years, and never received anything but kindness and encouragement from you fans."

The crowd stood silently still and then unstoppably applauded for two full minutes. According to the New York Times it was "the most astounding scene ever witnessed on a ball field."

Two years later, the Yankee hero was gone. His number (4) was the first ever-retired in Major League Baseball. He is in the Hall of Fame and the hall of hearts for every baseball fan that has ever loved spirit, class, and longevity.

WANTED

MORE PEOPLE LIKE
LUCILLE BALL
WHO MADE US LAUGH OUT LOUD
AND PIONEERED A STUDIO.

REWARDS
FOR THOSE WHO LOVE TO LAUGH

Why I Still Love Lucy

As soon as that big heart logo and lilting music signaled the beginning of the weekly program, people wanted to gather around the TV set for those crazy situations and rubber-faced reactions. Consider the Vitavegamin skit. Lucy stomping the grapes into wine. She and Ethel on that-ever speeding candy conveyer belt. Even in reruns, I defy you not to laugh.

However, her accomplishments extend beyond giggles. In many ways, she pioneered American-Latino relationships, women as studio leaders, and how to have a life after sitcoms.

Her show biz career started as a model, and progressed to forgettable movies (she was once dubbed the queen of the Bs). Two things changed that trajectory: she eloped with Cuban bandleader Desi Arnaz in 1940, and she found her niche as a comic actress in the late 1940s.

A breakthrough came in 1948, when she was cast as a wacky wife in *My Favorite Husband* for CBS radio. CBS saw the potential and wanted it developed for TV. Lucy's response: "Great ... but only with my husband Desi." CBS's response: "Yikes, we're not so sure America is ready for that." In defiance, Lucy launched a vaudeville act, where she acted like a zany housewife who always wanted to get into act of Arnaz's show. Result: laughter. Bigger result: CBS green-lighted the show.

In 1951, the show premiered and dominated for most of its run. She initiated the practice of filming before a live audience. She featured pregnancy in many episodes since it could not be hidden from the story lines (at age forty, she bore her first child, Lucy, and two years later, Desi Jr.).

In 1962, she became the first woman to run a major studio—Desilu. It was started as a joint venture with her husband, but after their 1960 divorce, she bought him out of the contract. In this capacity, she produced such hits as *Star Trek, Mission Impossible,* and *The Untouchables.*

And if that's not enough, she created two subsequent TV shows, starred in the Broadway show *Wildcat*, won four Emmy's, and was awarded the Lifetime Achievement Award from the Kennedy Center. And if all you want is a good laugh, rewatch the Lucy meets Harpo episode.

Oh My Gandhi!

The man was before my time. To be perfectly honest, he was before all of our times … especially since we now live in an era of confrontation, bully-driven knock-downs, bullets, domination, military weaponry, and terrorism.

For the prior 150 years, he was the most undeniable proof that passive resistance is actually the most effective way to achieve your goals. He invented civil disobedience. His tactic against the British government was often described as "noncooperation"—an apt term to describe the fact that he (and his millions of followers) would no longer buy British textiles, or participate in the ruse of government program.

It started in his early years as a twenty-four-year-old Indian in South Africa, when he was thrown off a train for riding in the "whites-only" department. Given the country and the times, it started as a nonviolent protest on behalf of Indians in South Africa.

After several years, he was invited back to India as a national hero. He immediately started to peacefully campaign for *Swanaj*, (translated for the Brits, "Quit India!") Make no mistake: his quest was not a piece of cake. He was jailed several times, suffered intense press criticism, and declared hunger strikes.

However (and this is key), the man never shot a bullet or incited any of his followers to do so. After decades of struggle, after WWII, there was Pyrrhic victory. In 1947, in acceptance of Gandhi's campaign for independence, Britain relinquished any claim to the territory. Bravo!

One year later, in acceptance of Hindu and Muslim warring factions, the area was divided along religious lines (the upper Muslim portion of Bangladesh and Pakistan) was officially separated from the larger portion of India. There was bloodshed. There was war.

It did not sit well with Gandhi. As was true with his entire life, he nonviolently campaigned against it. As he once said, "An eye for an eye only makes the whole world blind." Dare I report the circumstances of his blind end? He was violently shot with a bullet on the part of Muslim fundamentalists. What a loss!

The Enduring Steel of Young Malala

At what age does one become courageous? Your twenties? Midlife? As you move into your sunset years and figure, "What the hell, I may as well stand up for some damn principles"?

How about when you are in the seventh grade? Moreover, how does one stay brave after being critically injured and then aware there is a constant "contract" on her life?

That's the miraculous, steely strength of a young woman named Malala Yousafzai. Raised in the swat valley of Pakistan, she defied the Taliban as an eleven-year-old and demanded that girls be allowed to have an education. Her "sin"? She blogged for the BBC on this cause after many of her older classmates declined out of fear. To protect her safety, the BBC insisted she use a pseudonym (*Gul Makai*, or "Cornflower" in Urdu).

It didn't stop or fool the Taliban. On a bus ride home from school, several members boarded the bus, and shot her three times in the head. It left her in critical condition, and in a medically induced coma. A portion of her skull was removed, and she was ultimately transferred to a UK hospital where she recovered.

In the wake of this, would one not wish to find a tropical island and escape further pain? Not Malala. She became an even stronger advocate for the power of education, and her advocacy has grown into an international movement.

She has spoken before the United Nations, and at the ripe age of seventeen, she won the Nobel Peace Prize, and is still the youngest recipient of this honor. She was also recognized by Pakistan as one of their most amazing citizens and activists. In fact, fifty Islamic clerics did issue a *fatwa*—a ruling of Islamic law against the Islamic gunmen who tried to kill her.

In defiance, the Taliban to this day continue to call her a target.

And still she speaks out.

WANTED

MORE PEOPLE LIKE
MARIE CURIE
WHO DECIDED THAT 2 NOBEL PRIZES IN 2 FIELDS COULD BE DONE.

REWARDS
FOR THE ACHIEVERS

Multifaceted Marie

She must have been one brilliant person. Just as impressively, her academic achievements were in scientific fields largely dominated by men ... that is, until Marie entered the picture, and broke barriers that had heretofore been closed off to women.

Born in Poland, and later naturalized in France, she made her first mark in mathematics. She got her PhD in the field and became a professor at Krakow University. However, other sciences beckoned, and in 1891, she left to study physics in Paris.

Pierre Curie was her instructor in physics and chemistry, and the two attracted each other, at least partly due to their shared passion for science. (I've tried to imagine their first date, when they may have discussed William Roentgen's research on the existence of X-rays.) Within two years, the two simpatico brainiacs married, and eventually had two daughters.

After Marie gained an additional degree in physics, the couple began experimenting with radiology, along with physicist Henry Bequerel. For their breakthroughs in this field, they were awarded the Nobel Prize in 1903 (the first time a woman was so recognized). During that time, Marie published thirty-two scientific papers.

After her husband's death, she continued to explore the science of radiation, where she ultimately succeeded in repudiating the at-the-time accepted fact that an atom could never be split. She was awarded a second Nobel Prize for her work, this time in chemistry, making her the only woman to win two prizes in different disciplines. Just to add icing on the cake, she was the first woman to become a professor at the University of Paris.

In 1934, she passed away. It is widely presumed that her ailments were a result of her long-term exposure to radiation.

Throughout her life, she retained strong ties to her native Poland. She gave much of her Nobel Prize money to friends, family, students and research assistants, and refused to patent the radium isolation process so the scientific community to do its research unburdened. Albert Einstein called her "the only woman who could not be corrupted by fame." True, research and discovery were her things, not riches.

The Not-So-Dumb Blonde

In my early days of as a struggling actor, I remember asking one of my most trusted directors who he considered to be an amazing actress. "Marilyn Monroe," Jack Conner answered.

I think I spilled my drink. "Are you kidding, the blond bombshell?"

"First of all, she knew how to play the role. And she was capable of so much more."

Before I get ahead of myself, let me provide a brief précis of her early years. Born Norma Jean Mortensen, she began her career as a model, which led to a film contract at 20th Century Fox. In the 1950s and the 1960s, no woman was hotter. In 1952, she captured America's attention in *Asphalt Jungle* and *All about Eve*. In 1953, she gained her first leading role in *Niagara*. From there, it was a runaway train of hits—*Gentlemen Prefer Blondes*, *How to Marry a Millionaire*, *The Seven-Year Itch*, *Bus Stop*, and *The Misfits*.

There was an intervening event—the *Playboy* centerfold of December, 1953. Purloined from a nude photo taken in 1949, she became the first Playmate of the Month. It also spelled success for both *Playboy* and Marilyn Monroe, who never felt any need to apologize for her curves or exposure.

After a brief marriage in the mid-1940s, she began dating Joe DiMaggio, and married America's favorite ball player in 1954. Unfortunately, despite a passionate fiery relationship, they divorced in the same year. That's when the story becomes more convoluted. She began to reject her sexploitation image and enrolled in the Actor's Studio, run by Lee Strasburg, the progenitor of "method acting." According to Strasburg, "I have seen hundreds and hundreds of actors. Only two stand out. No. 1? Marlon Brando. No. 2? Marilyn Monroe."

After another brief marriage with playwright Arthur Miller, JFK was next. On May 1962, for his early birthday celebration, she sang a torchy "Happy Birthday, Mr., President" in a dress that had to be stitched around her body after the fitting. On August 5, 1962, she was dead. It was termed a "probably suicide" by the LA coroner, but conspiracy theorists continue to point fingers at JFK, RFK, the CIA, and the Mafia.

For the next twenty years, red roses were delivered to her grave every day, courtesy of Joe DiMaggio. Until this day, the world recognizes her as the quintessence of sexual allure, tease, and our deepest held-fantasies.

WANTED

MORE PEOPLE LIKE
MARK TWAIN
WHO COULD MAKE US SMILE AND THINK AT THE SAME TIME.

REWARDS
FOR ALL READERS

The King of Wit in America

As a Missouri native, I was always proud of Mark Twain. I remember visiting the small town of Hannibal and seeing the white fence that he used to entice his local buddies to restore the bright color, if they could only contribute a few pennies "for the privilege" of painting the spikes white.

What an amazing talent this man was! Yes, yes, yes … I know he used the n word in his early works. Consequently, in this world of "political correctness," he has been banned in many high schools across the nation. However, that was a rather common moniker before the civil war, and the man did become an advocate of abolition after 1860, and eventually became the greatest American humorist of the nation during the nineteenth century.

He was a versatile star. In his early days, he was a riverboat pilot on the Mississippi River. He was a speaker in men's clubs across the country. He travelled the world, and attempted through his cleverness and wit to outfox the millions of dollars of bad investments that he owed. After a year and a half overseas, he was clear of any debts.

Ultimately, he paid everything back to the people who believed in him and invested in him. He wrote *Tom Sawyer* and *Huckleberry Finn*. His first big hit (a short story) was "The Celebrated Jumping Frog of Calaveras County." He also wrote "A Tramp Abroad," "The Prince and the Pauper," and "Puddinhead Wilson."

In his later years, he toured the world and became a raconteur/stand-up comedian who represented this nation to the world.

A few of his potent quotes:

"If you tell the truth, you don't have to remember anything."

"Don't let schooling get in the way of your education."

"Humor is mankind's greatest blessing."

The man proved it over many decades. Thank you, Mark Twain.

WANTED

MORE PEOPLE LIKE

MUHAMMAD ALI

WHO GAVE UP THE BELT FOR PEACE

A.K.A.
THE GREATEST, THE LOUISVILLE LIP

REWARDS

FOR ALL CONSCIENTIOUS PEOPLE

The People's Champion

He was born Cassius Clay in Louisville, Kentucky, and began training for the boxing ring at age twelve. By the age of eighteen, he had won the Gold Medal in the Olympics … and by the age of twenty-two, he was the world champion of the heavyweight division, after a stunning defeat of Sonny Liston.

Always the showman, and cocky as can be, he predicted the knockout rounds of many of his fights, and taunted his opponents with criticism, poetry, and doggerel, such as "I will float like a butterfly and sting like a bee."

Most of America and the world absolutely loved the guy. In fact, he was named Sportsman of the Century by *Sports Illustrated*, and Sports Personality of the Century by the BBC. This, despite the fact that he converted to Islam in 1964, changed his name to Muhammad Ali, and later conscientiously objected to the war in Vietnam with the famous quote, "I got nothing against those Viet Cong."

As a result, he was stripped of his title during his prime boxing time, and spent the next four years lecturing on college campuses, and campaigning for peace without rancor or anger. His sentiment seemed to capture the sentiment of the times, especially coming from a brave man who was never afraid to throw a devastating punch and knock down an ugly opponent.

In 1971, the military decision was reversed by the Supreme Court. At the relatively ring-rusty age of twenty-nine, he climbed back in the ring and fought many of his best fights. There were four epic contests against Joe Frazier and George Foreman, including "The Fight of the Century," "The Rumble in the Jungle," and "Thrilla in Manila." C'mon, the guy did know how to package and promote a fight!

In the final analysis, Muhammad Ali was the only three-time linear Heavyweight Champion in the sport. (In 1964, 1974, and 1978, he was awarded the belt as the World Heavyweight Champion.) Despite his earlier reputation to dodge any punch, he later adopted a "rope-a-dope" technique that tired his opponents, and it gave him a late round advantage. Many brain surgeons suggest that that this nonstop pounding may have contributed to his Parkinson's disease.

However, we still love the guy, and always will. In the Golden Age of Heavyweights, he defeated every boxer in his era. According to *Ring Magazine*, he was ranked #1 in the Heavyweights of All Times. In 1996, he carried the torch and lit the flame for the Atlanta Olympics. For so many fans, he continues to hold out the light of promise and perseverance against adversity.

His Long Walk to Freedom

Nelson Mandela was a complex hero. He was a leader who preferred nonviolent protests but was not against more aggressive resistance to apartheid. He was an activist for Native African identity but was friendly with many white leaders around the world. He was a man who spent twenty-seven years in jail (often in hard labor) but retained his sunny, optimistic outlook for the future.

Through high school and college, the young man learned English studies and government but always had a keen interest in native African culture. In 1948, the National Party of South Africa codified and expanded racial segregation with new apartheid legislation. In defiance, Mandela organized boycotts and strikes. Within a few years, with his help, the ANC (African National Council) membership grew from twenty thousand to one hundred thousand. The government responded with mass arrests, and Mandela had to stand trial with twenty others. He was sentenced to nine months of hard labor.

In 1953, after opening his own law firm, he came to the opinion that the ANC had no alternative but more violent resistance to apartheid. Within a few years, he was arrested for "high treason" and inciting workers' strikes. Using the widely covered trial as a platform for political cause, he gave a three-hour opening speech but was ultimately sentenced to life in prison.

During his decades in various prisons, international resistance against apartheid grew. Banks stopped investing in South Africa. Violence escalated. Margaret Thatcher even asked authorities to release Mandela. Concerts in Wembley Stadium rallied popular support. Finally, in 1989, the newly elected national president, F. W. de Klerk announced that "apartheid is unsustainable." Eventually, he released all ANC prisoners, including Nelson Mandela, and shared a Nobel Peace Prize with Mandela in 1990.

In the country's first open election, Nelson Mandela was elected president of the country in 1994. He garnered 62 percent of the vote, and in an act of reconciliation, he named de Klerk his vice president. In his term, he assured that whites were protected and represented in "The Rainbow Nation."

The man promised he would only serve one term and kept that promise … becoming "the elder statesman" for a free South Africa and campaigning vigorously for racial equality and HIV research until he died in 2013 at the age of ninety-five. The world mourned for ten days. Hope and harmony gained an angel who must be proud of the progress. He will be celebrated for much longer.

The Queen of Empathy

She hosted the highest rated talk show in history. She is currently the only black billionaire in America. She is widely considered as the most influential woman in the world. She is also among the most generous Americans in the past one hundred years.

Her name is Oprah. Like many super-successful people, her path to glory had more than a few tough bumps in the road. Born in rural Mississippi, she was raised in poverty, raped at age nine, became pregnant at fourteen (the baby died in infancy). For a short time, she lived in Milwaukee, but then moved in with her father in Tennessee, who made education a priority. Something clicked at this stage of her life. She became an honors student, won an oratory contest, won the Miss Black Tennessee beauty pageant, and got a full college scholarship.

Within a few years, she landed the job on the lowest-rated talk show in Chicago. Within eight months, it was number one. Within a year, with the advice of her friend Roger Ebert, she syndicated the show, overtook Donahue, and became the most dominant talk show host for the next twenty-five years. Her secret? A warm, honestly curious, genuinely interested style.

Never one to rest on her laurels, she became a media mogul and Hollywood star in the next ten years. Her media credentials: she cofounded the television network Oxygen, became president of Harpo Productions (Oprah spelled backward), and established OWN, the Oprah Winfrey Network. In addition, she starred in *The Color Purple, Beloved, The Butler,* and *Selma* ... in addition to helping produce many of these features.

She is a true philanthropist. For ten years, she was named one of the fifty most generous Americans. In 2012, she donated four hundred full scholarships to Moorehouse College. She also established Oprah's Angel Network, and founded the Oprah Winfrey Leadership Academy for Girls on Henley on Kips, just south of Johannesburg.

Her private life is quite private. Shas had a thirty-year relationship with boyfriend Stedman Graham (they were once scheduled for a marriage, but that was called off). Her other long-time friends include Gayle King, Maria Shriver, and the late Maya Angelou, who she admired as an inspirational mentor, and "the rainbow of all cloudy days."

The Pope of the Slums

This guy was needed by more than a billion Catholics—a quiet, humble, courageous man who could remind the wavering Church population of its basic mission and concern for the poor.

He was not automatically destined to be the Vicar of Roman Catholicism. In his early days, he worked as chemical technician and even a bouncer. Hey, he even had a girlfriend in his younger days. In 1960, he was ordained as a Jesuit—widely considered as the most liberal, most education-oriented order of the priesthood (consider Notre Dame, Loyola Universities, St. Louis University, etc.).

After decades of prior Vatican scandals with priests and altar boys, the newly elected Pope Francis completely redirected the Church to interfaith dialogue, concern for the environment, and some tolerance of alternative lifestyles.

It started when he was the bishop of Buenos Aires, where he increased by 50 percent the Catholic presence in the slums, and created close ties with the Jewish community. Once elected to the papacy, he rejected the elegant papal apartments, and washed the feet of prisoners (both male and female) on his first Holy Thursday.

His has bigger outreach toward social and political causes. In his words, "If someone is gay and searching for the Lord, who am I to judge him?" He has condemned "war and hatred in the name of any God." He has called for environmental sanity. "We cannot continue to exploit our earth greedily, at the expense of the poor." He has even worked to ease the fifty-year tensions between the United States and Cuba. As a result of his talks with Raul Castro, the present leader of Cuba has issued a statement: "If the Pope continues this way, I will go back to praying and go back to church. I am not joking."

Just recently, the United Stated and Cuba agreed to have embassies in each country. Maybe tomorrow, Raul Castro will go the Church and say a prayer for peace and reconciliation. Perhaps we should all join him.

WANTED

MORE PEOPLE LIKE
PRINCESS DIANA
WHO EXUDED A COMMON TOUCH,
DESPITE A ROYAL PERCH.

A.K.A LADY DI
REWARDS
FOR REGULAR PEOPLE

The World's Princess

We barely knew her when Prince Charles proposed to the twenty-year kindergarten teacher in the early 1980s. From that very moment onward, the world's appetite for everything Diana was insatiable.

At first, she seemed shy and vulnerable. But at the fairy tale wedding of 1981, when we saw this beautiful woman so evidently in love, we wanted to participate in the storybook, but it was not destined to have a happy ending. By some accounts, Charles resumed his affair and affection with Camilla Parker-Bowles within the next twenty-four months. Queen Elizabeth and Prince Philip never seemed to embrace or enjoy Diana. And yet we continued to love Diana.

Throughout her sons' adolescence, she was widely recognized as an amazing, imaginative mother. At the same time, she also built up an atypical royal commitment to more modern charities and causes, including AIDS, leprosy, and the elimination of landmines.

Perhaps no divorce was ever more painful or public. The tabloids went on for years with recorded phone calls as testimony. Finally, in 1985, Prime Minister Major announced that the couple had decided to have an "amicable separation." At the same time, there was silence from the Buckingham Palace.

Just when we thought this once-royal human being might actually regain her footing, she met a tragic death on the Pont d'Almo road tunnel in Paris. She was travelling with Dodi Fayed (the son of Harrods's empire). Despite countless conspiracy theories, the crash was explained as a result of excessive drinking by the driver, perhaps aggravated by pursuing paparazzi.

The reaction from Buckingham Palace? None. The Queen was in her summer residence in Scotland at Balmoral Castle. Her decision not to immediately return to London, and her decision to not fly the royal standard at half-mast, was roundly criticized.

In retaliation, 2.5 billion people watched the funeral at Westminster Abbey. It was broadcast in 200 countries in forty-four languages. Elton John sang a version of "Candle in the Wind," and the world wept. Flowers were piled at Buckingham palace and every British embassy on the planet.

She was our princess, damn it. That's what the world seemed to say—at least most people outside the royal family.

The Whistle-Blower

It must be daunting to challenge Washington, D.C., the bureaucracy, and multimillion-dollar chemical industries about health risks and long-lasting dangers to the environment. And yet that's what Rachel Carson did throughout her entire life.

Her biggest claim to fame was the widely read tome, and Book-of-the Month Club selection titled *Silent Spring*, which alerted a nation about the powerful and often negative effects that we humans have on the natural world. But let me not get ahead of myself. The woman did have an illustrious career before her final publication.

She began her professional life as an aquatic biologist for the U.S. Bureau of Fisheries, and then became a full time writer in 1950. Her first big hit was *The Sea Around Us*, which plunged the depths of marine environmentalism and the dangers that threatened healthy oceans. In the '50s, her interest turned to the ecology of our daily lives. She was particularly concerned with problems related to synthetic pesticides, and the damaging effects that unbridled DDT might have on birds, crops, and our own eventual existence as part of the food chain. With frequent speeches, radio broadcasts, college lectures, and even a few documentary films, she made a very convincing case that we humans were endangering our own future.

Surprise, surprise! The chemical companies did *not* really appreciate her alarm bell. DuPont (the main originator of DDT) and Velsicol Chemical Company (the exclusive manufacturer of Chlordane) threatened legal action, unless Houghton-Mifflin and the New Yorker ceased publication of the book and newspaper chapters.

In rebuttal, Rachel accused the chemical companies of deliberately spreading untruths, and public officials of blindly accepting industry claims of safety. Despite the encroaching damaging effects of cancer, she published the landmark book in 1963, partly as a reference to our rather dodgy future, and to the absence of birdsongs as a result of pesticides.

The groundbreaking pioneer had a decades-long relationship with a woman named Dorothy Freeman. Perhaps it was just a shared interest in intellectual pursuits or the environment; after all, Ms. Freeman was married, and she shared many of her letters with her husband. After Carson's death, hundreds of letters between the women were destroyed, so we will never know. Evidently, that's was the way both women wanted it.

As the most public eco-advocate, perhaps it is only fitting to respect the woman's dying request for a forever-private life.

Deigen Me Jugar a La Pelota

In his native home of Puerto Rico, it was every umpire's command to begin the game. "Let's play ball."

Despite his humble beginnings as the son of a poor farmer, Roberto Clemente always seemed to have a talent for hitting the baseball.

In 1954, he was first choice for the rookie draft, and he was signed by the Pittsburgh Pirates. From that day forward, it was a meteoric rise. But before we get into the amazing stats, let's at least acknowledge the barriers that this athlete faced. He suffered under a triple whammy of prejudice. He was the first ever Latino player to break into the major leagues. With his African heritage, he also appeared black, and there were less than 10 African-Americans in the league. Third, unlike every other ball player, he spoke Spanish.

Okay. Let's get to the numbers. This guy was a true superstar. He played eighteen seasons for the Pirates. He was an All-Star in twelve of those seasons. He was the NL batting champ four times, and the NL Most Valuable Player. He won the Golden Glove award for twelve years. Perhaps most impressively, in the 1960s, he batted over .300 for nine out of ten seasons. (In his "bad season"? He hit .291.) From a poetic standpoint, I also love this sad fluke of an achievement: he got his 3,000th at his last major league at bat.

Why cut it this close? It was an accident. Roberto Clemente had agreed to fly to Nicaragua after an earthquake to deliver aid to the victims. Unfortunately, the plane didn't make it. Six months later, he was the first Latino inducted into the Hall of Fame, and the first ever to be honored with a precedent that, if deceased, one would not need to endure the five-year "inductee waiting period."

He was a very proud player, married with three children, and a hero in all of Latin America. Three hundred thousand Puerto Rican signatures saluted him in his last game at Forbes Field. In 1961, he and Orlando Cepeda came back to Puerto Rico and greeted more than a hundred thousand baseball fans.

As of last year, 27.3 percent of all Major League ball players were Latino. However, before there was a second one to pioneer the league, there was only one Roberto Clemente.

"Let's play ball."

This One's for the Gipper

The man was often underestimated. After all, a B-movie actor wanting to be the leader of the free world? And yet he succeeded in changing the economic landscape, helped bring about the end of the Cold War, and became an ideological icon for decades of conservatives.

You wouldn't predict it from his early years in broadcasting and film. His initial jobs were in small town radio stations. The biggest feather in his cap? In Des Moines, Iowa, he announced Chicago Cub games from the tickertape data as it were a live game. In 1937, he got a seven-year contract from Warner Brothers. Despite his good looks and genial charm, he was relegated to the B-film unit for the first few years, including *Knute Rockne, All American* and *Bedtime for Bonzo*. His enlistment into the army for WWII interrupted any Hollywood momentum he might have had.

After the war, he was elected president of the Screen Actors Guild, and reelected to seven additional one-year terms. At the time, he was a Democrat (and even campaigned for Truman), but as his life had changed, so did his politics. He voted for Ike, married Nancy, and became the host of the GE Theatre. Part of his contract required him to tour G.E. plants sixteen weeks every year, and often demanded fourteen speeches a day. In 1962, he officially changed parties and became a Republican.

In 1966, he ran for governor of California with the famous quote, "Send the welfare bums back to work." He won over two-time governor Edmund "Pat" Brown, and was reelected four years later. Consequently, many Republican conservatives began touting him for national office. In fact, in 1976, he came close, narrowly losing to Gerald Ford 1187–1070 electoral votes. Four years later, it was his time. Running against Jimmy Carter, he projected a prouder, more confident America … and carried forty-four states.

In his first term, he fired all the striking Air Traffic controllers, after warning them to report within forty-eight hours, which sent the message: this guy is not kidding around. He introduced a thing derisively called "Reaganomics" which decreased unemployment from 7.5 to 5.4. He also lowered the top tax rate from 70 percent to 50 percent and the lowest rate from 14 percent to 11 percent.

Four years later, the campaign commercial "It's Morning in America" helped remind voters that they liked the guy's performance. He carried forty-nine states. His second term was more dominated by international politics. On the heels of his "Star Wars" defense system, the Soviet Union began outspending their budgets just to stay competitive. Indeed, he called them "the evil empire," but did have four summit meetings with Mikhail Gorbachev. His most famous challenge was in a speech he gave in Berlin, where he admonished the Russian leader and said, "Mr. Gorbachev, tear down this wall!"

WANTED

MORE PEOPLE LIKE
ROSA PARKS
WHO REFUSED TO TAKE A BACK SEAT TO ANYONE.

REWARDS
FOR THE CONFIDENT

Rosa and the Bus

For those of us who lived most of our lives in the second part of the twentieth century, it's jarring to know how humiliating the overt prejudice against blacks must have been.

Consider this: In 1955, 75 percent of all bus riders in Montgomery, Alabama were African-American, or as they were called in the day, "coloreds." However, the first four rows of all busses were reserved for white people. The colored section started at from the fifth row and beyond. Wait, it gets worse! If by chance there were a few extra white people who got on the bus ride, the driver could move the colored sign back a few rows, and order the already-seated African-Americans to give up their seat to the "more entitled" white people.

That never sat well with Rosa Parks, a hard-working seamstress in Montgomery. Yes, she had joined the NAACP earlier, but had never been a known activist. However, on this particular day, she decided she would not sit at the back of the bus. Instead, she moved to the window seat … and allowed two other bus seats for the incoming white patrons. She later explained that her actions were spontaneous. According to her, "the bus was the first way I realized there was a black world and a white world."

She was arrested and convicted of violating the laws of segregation, known as Jim Crow laws.

Result: a young Martin Luther King Jr. and Edgar Nixon, the president of the NAACP came to her aid. Black residents boycotted for 381 days in Montgomery, Alabama. On the heels of this, the U.S. Supreme Court ruled that the segregation laws were unconstitutional. Oh, and one more thing. Rosa was fired from her job as a seamstress, and received numerous death threats.

Eventually, she moved to Detroit with her family to restart her life. For many years, she worked for Congressman John Conyers in Michigan. To this day, many call her "the First Lady of Civil Rights."

Why do it? In her own words: "I knew I had the strength of my ancestors with me."

The Triumph of One Man's Will

Look at a star in the heavens tonight, and try to define where it came from, how it was created, when it will end, and what relationship it may have with other stars that we cannot even see. Chances are we would just make a wish and move on. Unlike us, Stephen Hawking wanted answers, and despite the fact that he is now incapable of speaking, walking, even smiling ... he continues to move on.

Always a gifted student, he was diagnosed with ALS (Lou Gehrig disease) in his senior year at Oxford ... about the time he met Jane Wilde, and proposed marriage. Despite the fact that doctors only gave him two years to live, they did wed, sired three kids ... and both intellectually endowed parents made their marks in their scientific fields.

In many ways, Stephen's path was more challenging. In the '60s, his physical condition declined. He started using crutches, and he ended his lectures. He slowly lost his ability to write. In the 1970s, his speech deteriorated to the point that only his family and close friends could understand his slurred speech. In 1985, he contracted pneumonia, which resulted in a tracheotomy. What was ever left of his speech was removed and he required three shifts of round-the-clock nurses a day.

This could not have been easy for his wife, Jane. In the late '70s, she found comfort with the church organist, but would not leave Stephen, who accepted the relationship, given the circumstances. However, in the late 1980s, Hawking became attached to one of his nurses, and moved out of the house in 1990. (Hey, nobody's perfect.) In 1995, he divorced Jane, and married Elaine, his nurse ... alienating all of his children. Explanation, according to Hawking: "I am a scientist first, a popular science writer second, and in all ways and manners, a normal human being with same drives, dreams, desires, and ambitions as the next person."

In fact, Hawking has tried his best to bypass his disability (which continues to upset many paraplegic advocates), and pursue the glory of science. I admit that I barely understand his intellectual pursuits. His first book *(A Brief History of Time)* was published by Bantam Press in 1984, despite a contentious battle with the publisher who wanted him to "simplify, simplify, simplify," which just irritated the cantankerous Hawking all the more. In the final analysis, Bantam prevailed and the book sold over nine million copies. Subsequently, he published even simpler books—*The Universe in a Nutshell* (for kids) and *A Briefer History of Time*.

Today, Hawking communicates via one remaining nerve ending in his cheek, which translates his thoughts at one word a minute. He has fostered research that may enable a brain-to-translation process. After his divorce from Elaine, he has regained healthy contact with Jane and his three children. And he refuses to retire. Perhaps when he looks at the stars, he still wonders.

The Man Who Taught Us to Think Differently

I have seen many CEOs walk across the stage. They are usually wearing Brooks Brothers navy blue suits with cufflinks and a pocket square. However, one was very different. He would stroll across the platform wearing a mock turtleneck, Levi's 501 jeans, and New Balance 991 sneakers.

His name was Steve Jobs, and he did more to redefine the personal computer business, animated movies, music, phones, tablets, and retail than any other leader in the past century.

Adopted as a young baby in San Francisco, he always had an interest in tech and electronics. After dropping out of Reed College, he and his wiz buddy, Steve Wozniak, founded Apple in 1976. Positioned against the corporate juggernauts like IBM and Hewlett-Packard, Apple had a real niche—the personal computer. In 1984, he introduced the zoomy, colorful Macintosh, which gained all kinds of headlines and publicity.

However, he was a brash young man, and he was forced out of the company in 1985. While the company then struggled, Jobs founded NeXT, a computer platform for higher education. He also formed an alliance with George Lucas and cofounded Pixar, which Disney eventually bought for 7.4 billion dollars, and which made him one of their most celebrated board members.

In 1997, Apple was almost bankrupt. In an act of desperation, they bought Jobs's NeXT company for more millions, and asked him to come back home. Taking a salary of $1 a year, Jobs did so and helped turn to company to profitability in one year's time. That's when they launched the campaign called "Think Different." And then the new CEO made good on that promise—by introducing the iMac, iTunes, the iPod, the iPad, and the most highly-regarded, service-friendly retail stores in America.

Today, Apple is one of the most profitable companies in the world.

Unfortunately, Steve Jobs was unable to see the full fruition of his dreams. He was diagnosed with pancreatic cancer in his early 50s, and died of complications in 2011. However, as I type this on my Apple desktop, carry an Apple laptop to Europe, make calls on my iPhone and listen to my favorite hits on iTunes, I am well aware of the lasting influence he has on millions of our lives.

Mr. Blockbuster

So many people I have studied in this pursuit have discovered their true talents later in life after some struggles. Steven Spielberg was not such a late bloomer. From his early teens, he seemed to know what he wanted to do and did it with such aplomb and accolades.

At the age of sixteen, he wrote and directed his first independent film called *Firelight*. On the basis of this twenty-six-minute indie film (which his dad funded), the kid got a seven-year contract with Universal Studios—the youngest one ever to do so.

On the heels of this, he did four so-so films, including *Sugarland Express* that did get good directorial reviews. And then came *Jaws*—which merited three Academy Awards for editing, score, and sound. Oh, by the way, it also grossed $470 million at the box office.

It was just a prelude to amazing success:

Poltergeist
The Twilight Zone
The Goonies
Indiana Jones Trilogy
Batman
Hook
Jurassic Park

And then the maestro departed from sci-fi and created amazing humanistic film:

Schindler's List
Saving Private Ryan
Catch Me If You Can
Interstellar
Lincoln

Along the way, he created DreamWorks and produced *Titanic* and dozens of amazing computer-generated classics. He has won three Oscars. He's been nominated seven times. And he's not done yet.

I, for one, will attend any movie he produces or directs. He has a gift. I simply want to experience it.

WANTED

MORE PEOPLE LIKE
THEODORE ROOSEVELT
WHO MIXED COWBOY, CHARISMA, AND CLASS MORE THAN ANY OTHER LEADER.

A.K.A. TEDDY
REWARDS
FOR ALL MULTI-DIMENSIONAL PEOPLE.

Cowboy or President? Both!

There has never been a more contradictory (and perhaps more interesting) president. Born a very sickly child with asthma, he became a macho man. Despite his family wealth—he was born in a Manhattan brownstone, and his father helped form the Metropolitan Museum of Art—Theodore Roosevelt became the most "trust-busting" president in American history. Despite his naturalist penchant to save national parks and forests, he loved going on safaris to hunt big game. Throughout most of his life, he was a beloved figure in American politics, even though he jettisoned the Republican Party in his later years.

Theodore was a man who seemed to be equally comfortable bouncing back and forth between public service and a life of adventure. After serving as a New York State assemblyman, at which time his wife and mother died within twelve hours, he found solace operating a cattle ranch in the Dakotas. He served as the assistant secretary of the navy but resigned after one year to form the Rough Riders for the war in Cuba. Returning as a war hero, he was elected governor of New York in 1898. In 1900, he was elected vice president under McKinley, who was soon assassinated, making Teddy the youngest president in American history at forty-two years old.

In his two terms, he broke up the largest railroad and the largest oil company. He established the Meat Inspection Act and the Pure Food and Drug Act. He established a movement called the Square Deal, which appealed to the middle class and underclass of America. His biggest foreign policy? The Panama Canal, which was his pet project to open up trade in the Americas.

After two terms, he groomed Taft. He then went on an African safari, where he bagged elephants, rhinos, and other rare species—to be brought back to the Museum of Natural History.

In 1912, disappointed with Taft and rejected by the Republicans, he formed the Bull Moose party and ran again for president. An apocryphal story of that campaign: there was an assassination attempt on Teddy. Undeterred, the man delivered the speech with blood oozing out of his white shirt. What a guy!

He did not win the election but went on a two-year expedition on the Amazon. It was a tough trip, and he did suffer some injuries and eventually succumbed to complications. However, along the way I can only imagine that Teddy was smiling at the wondrous nature and adventure of the expedition.

The Father of Mickey Mouse

Like so many success stories, the empire started with many years of ups and downs.

Born in Chicago and raised in Missouri, Walt Disney seemed to always have a childlike fascination for animation and cartoons, but his journey to cultural icon took a few twists and turns. After some unsuccessful ventures, he set up a studio called Laugh-O-Gram in Kansas City, which went bankrupt. With a suitcase and $20, he and his brother Roy decided to head to Hollywood and try their luck in the America's film capital.

After some Alice and Oswald the Lucky Rabbit cartoons, the man finally settled on a character called Mickey Mouse. His first few efforts were silent films, but when Steamboat Willie came out with sound, it was an instant hit. (Walt himself was the mouse's voice until 1947.) He followed this with *Three Little Pigs*, which ran for months in movie theaters, thanks to the song "Who's Afraid of the Big Bad Wolf." Still short of cash, he had to fund his first full-length movie *Snow White and the Seven Dwarfs* by showing it to creditors first. It became the most successful movie of 1938.

From that point, he had an amazing string of hits. *Pinocchio, Fantasia, Bambi, Alice in Wonderland, Peter Pan, Cinderella*. Along the way, Mickey, Donald Duck, Goofy, Pluto, and other characters became household names. In time he added live-action films to his portfolio—including *Old Yeller*, *Pollyanna*, and *The Parent Trap*. The films were beloved by Americana and by the Academy of Arts and Sciences. In fact, his movies won twenty-two Oscars and were nominated fifty-nine times. Walt himself won more awards and nominations than any other individual in history.

As magical and surprising as all these movies were, his interest in theme parks was just as imaginative. Opened in 1956, the place was called Disneyland and was unlike any so-called amusement park that had ever been devised. It had discrete sections or "neighborhoods." It had castles and characters. It had quality. Leaving no stone unturned, Disney entered television with the studio's first daily TV show, *The Mickey Mouse Club*. It started in 1955 and continued into the '90s.

Walt did envision Disney World and Epcot Center in Orlando to captivate even more audiences. However, in 1966, ill health claimed the man before the parks opened. However, even after his death, the empire continues to grow and evolve. Along came Disneyland in Paris, Tokyo Disney Resort, and Hong Kong Disneyland. All thrive.

As they used to sing on *The Mickey Mouse Club*, "Forever let us hold our banner high. Come along, sing our song, and join the jamboree. M-I-C-K-E-Y … M-O-U-S-E." It seems clear that millions of dreamers in the world still wish to join the club.

WANTED

MORE PEOPLE LIKE
WINSTON CHURCHILL
WHO REFUSED TO CONSIDER DEFEAT.

REWARDS
FOR THE SPIRITED

The Man Who Would Never Surrender

He is considered the most persuasive force against Nazi Germany and the one person who rallied the Allied forces to win World War II.

Born of a charismatic British politician and an American socialite mother, Winston Churchill bounced between politics and military service in his early years. As a young man, he was engaged in conflicts in Cuba and India and fought in the Boer War in South Africa. As early as 1900, he won a seat in parliament and enjoyed the opportunity to shape policy for an entire nation. At some points, he would rejoin the army and then regain votes in his parliamentary districts. Back and forth.

Undoubtedly as a result of this dual experience, he had a very clear vision of the global unrest, along with the opportunities and responsibilities of the United Kingdom. He was one of the first to recognize the threat of Adolf Hitler in the 1930s. In speeches and radio broadcasts, he warned the nation of this danger—not just for the Jews in Germany but also for the entire continent. A master of oratory, he was able to object on moral grounds and marshal support in Great Britain. In one of his famous speeches, he juxtaposed Prime Minister Neville Chamberlain's indecisive dilemma as one of "war or shame." In a matter of months, Chamberlain was gone, and Winston Churchill was named the new prime minister of Great Britain.

Almost at once, he stood alone against the atrocities of Adolf Hitler. As the Nazi rolled, he gained more international support. When Germany advanced in France and the Low Countries, he gave one of his most inspirational speeches. In it, he promised the British listeners that "if we last a thousand years, this will be our finest hour."

Once America joined the war after the attack on Pearl Harbor, he had a kindred spirit in Franklin Roosevelt. Evidently, from 1939 to1945, the two men exchanged one thousand seven hundred letters and telegrams and met eleven times. A hardened anticommunist, he also supported Stalin's entry into the war, judging it the "lesser of two evils."

After VE day, and VJ day, Churchill was shockingly voted out of office. The most popular theory? The Brits felt he was the perfect choice for a World War, but not the right guy for rebuilding peace. In four years, the citizens reconsidered their opinion and reelected him to second term as prime minister in 1950.

In 1953, he won a Nobel Prize in literature for his six-book series on WWII. According to the Nobel congratulations, it was awarded in honor of his ability to "defend exalted human values." He was the first person ever given an honorary citizenship in the USA. In 2002, he was named the greatest Briton of all times in a UK poll.